Sneaky Piecing

Beth's 20+ Tips, Tricks & Techniques
for Cutting, Stitching, Pressing, Finishing
& More • 6 Quilt Projects

Beth Ferrier

C&T PUBLISHING

Photography and Artwork copyright © 2012 by C&T Publishing, Inc.

PUBLISHER: Amy Marson

CREATIVE DIRECTOR: Gailen Runge

ART DIRECTOR: Kristy Zacharias

EDITORS: Cynthia Bix and Phyllis Elving

TECHNICAL EDITORS: Teresa Stroin and Priscilla Read

COVER/BOOK DESIGNER: April Mostek

PRODUCTION COORDINATOR: Jenny Davis

PRODUCTION EDITOR: S. Michele Fry

ILLUSTRATOR: Valyrie Friedman

Photography by Christina Carty-Francis and Diane Pedersen
of C&T Publishing, Inc., unless otherwise noted

Published by C&T Publishing, Inc., P.O. Box 1456, Lafayette, CA 94549

Library of Congress Cataloging-in-Publication Data

Ferrier, Beth.

Sneaky piecing : Beth's 20+ tips, tricks & techniques for cutting, stitching, pressing, finishing & more - 6 quilt projects / Beth Ferrier.

pages cm

ISBN 978-1-60705-628-7 (soft cover)

1. Patchwork--Patterns. 2. Quilting--Patterns. I. Title.

TT835.F475 2012

746.46'041--dc23

2012013359

Printed in China

10 9 8 7 6 5 4 3 2 1

dedication

To Kent, who has always been my safe place to land

acknowledgments

Many times in my life I have been blessed to have just the right person show up with just the help I have needed to grow and mature. I like to think of these people as my angels with skin on. They have been teachers and friends. There have even been chance encounters with strangers. For them, I will be forever grateful. We truly are the sum of all who have loved us.

Special thanks go to Karen Boutte, the best BFF ever, for talking me in from the ledge, *again*; to Cyndi Hershey at Red Rooster Fabrics and Patti Carey at Northcott Silk for their generous additions to my fabric stash; to the wonderful folks at Floriani Embroidery, whose thread was used for most of the quilting; and, of course, to the crew at C&T—what a joy to work with you!

contents

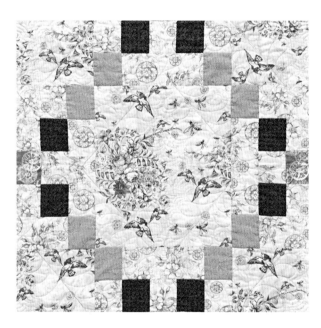

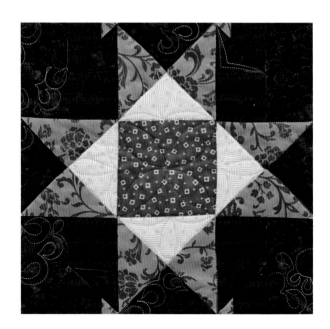

introduction

In my universe there is no such thing as one right way to do things. The right way is the way that gives us the outcome we want. I never argue with success. Sure, there may be easier ways, but those ways will be different for each quilter.

What I offer in this book is purely information. It's not meant to be the last word on how anything should be done. It calls no judgment on those who suggest just the opposite. Instead, simply think of these "sneaky piecing tricks" as additional tools for your quilting toolbox. Someday a technique that has always worked for you may let you down; perhaps something you see here will be just the right solution.

Many of us just picked up the tools and started making quilts, without any real instruction, and we've made it work. But I've learned some strategies over my (mumble mumble mumble) decades of quiltmaking that I'd like to share. We'll start simply, beginning with the very basics of cutting, sewing, and pressing. Then I'll explain how to exploit those skills to make piecing more fun and successful. The projects in this book have been designed to give you the opportunity to put your newfound (or newly refreshed) piecing strategies to work, building from basic straight seams to more complex and exciting shapes.

Although I don't think of myself as naturally organized, I do like putting things in order. More than anything, I hate looking for stuff. I'm sort of an anti-packrat. If I don't have a place for it, out it goes. (I'm not saying that everything is always in its place, just that it has a place.) Being organized (even just a little bit) gives me so much more time to sew. In this book, you'll find tons of little organizing tips to help you get the most out of your sewing time.

I also love to create systems—orderly little processes that allow me to relax into my projects without constantly checking and rechecking. I call this "thinking once." You'll see fun strategies for this sprinkled throughout the book.

measure twice, cut once

When I started seriously quilting in 1980, I was a stay-at-home mom. Money was tight. For close to fifteen years, I used nothing more than a 6″ × 12″ ruler and a generic rotary cutter to cut out my quilt pieces. Worse, instead of a self-healing mat, I used the Formica sink cutout left over from our kitchen remodel. No wonder the blades went dull so quickly! Penny wise and pound foolish, that was. Eventually it dawned on me that having the right tool for the job would make the process easier—and lots more fun.

During the second fifteen years of my quilting life, I have hoarded my pennies, used coupons, and shopped the sales to build up my arsenal of quilting tools. I've brought home tools that have become favorites, as well as more than a few that have fallen into the "What was I thinking?" category.

We can learn from the old carpenter's motto of measuring twice before cutting once. Careful attention to detail at the start of a project will make the rest of the process much more enjoyable. So let's take a few minutes to talk about our tools.

Beth says:

"Well begun is well done."

Tools of the Trade

The tools we need for pieced quilts are pretty basic: fabric (of course), rulers and rotary cutters, and—for heaven's sake—a self-healing mat. Let's start with fabric.

Fabrics

We don't often think of fabric as one of our tools, but it is! Just as a carpenter learns the characteristics of each type of wood in order to choose what's best suited to a project, our fabric choices can ultimately determine the success of our quilts.

For the best results, use the best materials that you can afford. Beginners often cringe at the cost of quilt-shop fabric, turning instead to what can be found relatively cheaply at chain stores. The problem is, sewing with poorly made fabric can suck all the joy out of piecing a quilt. Inexpensive fabric may be loosely woven, resulting in pieces that stretch out of shape easily. Fabric is made up of warp thread (parallel to the selvage) and weft thread (perpendicular to the selvage). In lower-quality fabric, these two threads are often of different thicknesses, which can cause them to shrink disproportionately. Have you ever applied a steamy hot iron to a fabric square, only to lift the iron and discover that you now have a rectangle rather than a square? The difference in thread is the reason.

I'm not saying that you shouldn't use cheaper fabric. But understanding the nature of your fabric will help you to be more successful with the choices you make.

To wash or not to wash

For the most part, I am a member of the great unwashed. Unwashed fabric is firm and crisp, which I believe makes for easier machine piecing. By comparison, washed fabric is soft and much nicer for handwork.

That said, if I fall in love with a fabric of questionable pedigree, I wash it and toss it into a hot dryer until it's bone dry. I like to get all of its potential bad behavior over and done with before I start cutting. And yes, I mix washed and unwashed fabrics in the same project.

Prewashing, however, doesn't guarantee that colors won't continue to run. The transfer of dye is as much a function of a receptive fabric as of a running color. That's how color catchers work—they are simply receptive fabrics. An easy way to test colorfastness is to toss bits of your project's fabric together into warm, sudsy water. (I like to sew the bits together before doing this, so I can see how the seams will react.) Swish the fabric around and see what happens. Rinse and dry with an iron or in the dryer. Then repeat. If color runs, you can decide whether you want to get rid of the runner or the receiver.

cheating allowed!

sneaky piecing tricks

For some quilters, choosing fabric for a project is the scary part. If you struggle with fabric decisions, here's a trick that might help you. It starts with a "cheater."

"What's a cheater?" you ask. (I heard you!) Simply put, a cheater is a chunk of fabric that has the colors and feel you'd like for your project. Not to be confused with what's often referred to as cheater cloth (preprinted panels that mimic piecing), this cheater is a touchstone for your project. The piece may never actually appear in the quilt, but if each chosen fabric coordinates with it, they'll all play together like lifelong friends.

The cheater can be as small as a fat quarter or, if you really love it, big enough for the quilt back, with maybe even a couple extra yards for pillowcases and window treatments.

When shopping for fabric, pile the bolts on the counter and look at the edges. Unless you're making a quilt with large pieces, seeing the fabric in wide swatches can be misleading. Looking at the stack from the side is a better representation of what you'll see in the quilt.

Place the cheater fabric on top and let it drape over one end. This will show you how well the cheater plays with the other fabrics. Use the cheater colors as a starting point. *No matching!* Instead, choose lighter or darker shades.

Drape your cheater over the stack of fabrics.

I think of it as inviting friends to a party. Great conversation needs different points of view, but no fighting! Prints in different scales, geometrics, and colors that aren't in the original cheater will make for an interesting quilt.

smart use of grainline

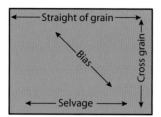
Fabric has three types of grain: straight of grain (sometimes called "length of grain" or "lengthwise grain"), cross grain, and bias.

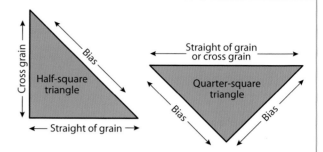

When we make "width of fabric" cuts, we're cutting across the grain. The *cross grain* runs the length of our strips, perpendicular to the selvage. Grab a bit of fabric and stretch it, selvage to selvage; the cross grain has some give. I like to use cross-grain strips for bindings. That bit of stretch lets me put a little tension on the outer edges, resulting in a nice, tidy finish.

The *bias* runs at a 45° angle to the cross grain or the straight of grain. It's really stretchy. We take advantage of this when cutting bias strips for binding scalloped edges or creating curvaceous stems for appliqué. But bias edges can cause all sorts of problems. If not handled respectfully, they can be distorted easily.

Traditional quilting uses lots of right-angle triangles, often referred to as half-square or quarter-square triangles. In half-square triangles, the bias edge falls on the long side of the triangle; quarter-square triangles have the bias on the short sides. Planning to stitch the bias edges as early in the construction as possible helps us avoid stretching the pieces out of shape.

The *straight of grain* runs parallel to the selvage and is the strongest grain. We can cut fabric to take advantage of this. Any time a project uses rectangles, I cut them so that the long side is on the straight of grain. For example, *Make Mine Argyle* (page 59) has *lots* of rectangles. Consider this quilt's 3″ × 9½″ rectangles. We could easily cut a 3″-wide strip and subcut that into 9½″ segments. But that would put the stretchy cross grain along the length of the rectangles. That's great for easing, but easing results in misshapen blocks. Instead, if we cut the strip 9½″ wide and subcut it into 3″ segments, we end up with the sturdiest grainline along the length of the rectangles.

Careful planning puts the long side on the straight grain.

Fabric collections

Choosing fabrics from a single collection can be tempting. Manufacturers and designers seemingly have done all the work for us, creating perfectly coordinated choices.

Some collections are quite good, with a lovely range of light, medium, and dark, as well as prints in different sizes. Many collections, though, end up being terribly matchy-matchy and mostly medium. In fact, about 80 percent of the fabrics in quilt shops are medium value.

Mix it up, invite the quirky auntie to the party, have a little fun. Above all, remember that this is *your* quilt. All that really matters is that you are pleased with your choices.

Beth says:

"A quilt that is all medium is neither rare nor well done."

Rotary Cutters

Rotary cutters come in all sizes, shapes, and colors. Manufacturers are working feverishly to create the perfect cutter. When I travel to the twice-yearly International Quilt Market (the wholesale show for the quilting industry), I am always on the lookout for innovative tools. That said, my favorite rotary cutter remains the plain old straight Olfa.

About the blades

Rotary cutters come out of the package with the blades tightened down for travel, so you have to loosen them before you can cut. Honestly, folks, the blade is supposed to roll!

Hold the cutter loosely with two fingers by the end of the handle, blade extended. The blade should roll easily on the mat, with no drag. If it doesn't, loosen the blade until it rolls freely, but not so much that it wobbles. Be careful the first few times you cut with a newly loosened blade. It may feel a little like stepping onto ice.

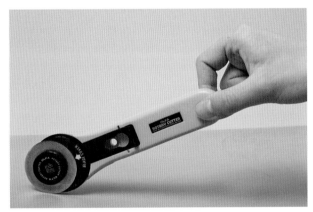

Hold the cutter loosely to check that it rolls easily.

Change your blade often—a dull blade just makes you work harder and can make a mess of your cutting mat. If you notice a bubble of fabric rising in front of the blade as you cut, it's a sure sign that the blade should have been changed several projects ago.

Cutting technique

Many of us just pick up a rotary cutter and have at it, without any real instruction. I never argue with success, so if what you're doing is working for you, feel free to skip to the next section. But if you'd like to be able to cut better and for longer, play along with me here.

Many times, we may grab the rotary cutter and grip it in our fists; in fact, the shapes of

Holding the cutter like this will make your job harder.

some rotary cutters even encourage this grip. But consider what this way of cutting does to our posture.

Try it with me! Notice that when you cut straight away from yourself using this grip, your wrist is contorted, your shoulders are hunched, and your elbow is akimbo. You're using the weaker muscles in the forearm. You have to twist your body to cut straight, forcing you to lean forward to complete the cut.

Yikes! No wonder we are always looking for an easier way to cut out our quilts.

Now try this. Rest the end of the rotary cutter against the heel of your

In the correct grip, the forefinger is extended.

palm. Extend your forefinger so that it rests on the notches on the handle. Feel how the cutter has become an extension of the arm? The wrist is in a neutral position, the shoulder is relaxed, and the elbow is close to the body. The arm now works like a piston, with the upper arm muscles pushing the cutter forward. The forefinger is just a guide. You no longer have to twist to cut straight. Your reach is extended—no bending required!

When you cut, don't place your palm flat on the ruler. Instead, hold your palm up, spider-like, with two fingers (your pointer and middle fingers) and your thumb on the ruler and two fingers (the ring and baby fingers) off the ruler on

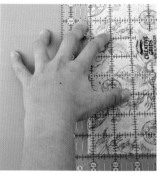

Use a spiderlike hand position to hold the ruler steady.

the side *opposite* where you'll cut. This hand position will stop the ruler from sliding, keep your thumb out of the cutter's path, and protect your wrist from repetitive strain injury.

When cutting with longer rulers, spider-walk your hand up the ruler to keep it positioned near the rotary cutter. As the cutter passes your ruler hand, pause in your cutting, carefully walk your fingers a few inches toward the far end of the ruler, and resume cutting.

cutting two-handed

sneaky piecing tricks

No matter how you lay out your fabric, sooner or later it's going to be in the wrong position for your strong hand. Learning to cut with your nondominant hand will increase accuracy and efficiency. It saves me tons of time being able to clean up raw edges with my left hand and then resume cutting with my right hand without having to shift the fabric. It takes practice, but that's true of pretty much anything worth doing.

The blade should always be flush against the ruler. A straight cutter can easily flip from hand to hand, whereas shaped rotary cutters don't allow you to cut with either hand. Pretty much any blade that extends down instead of forward is one-handed only.

Take care!

Some quilters seem to take a perverse pride in bucking the idea of always closing their cutters. Let me tell you, these suckers are super sharp—we pay extra for that sharpness. It takes just the slightest touch to draw blood, and heaven forbid that an open cutter gets dropped on a bare foot.

I'm not a big fan of cutters with automatic guards. Unless the guard is locked each time the cutter is put down, we can count on it to automatically retract whether it is against fabric or our body. And the guard usually just adds to the drag on our fabric, making us work harder.

Rulers

Although my repertoire has seriously expanded beyond that beloved first ruler, the 6½″ × 12½″ remains my go-to tool. I try to use the smallest ruler possible to cut fabric because this gives me less tool to control. For basic strip cutting, a 6½″ × 12½″ ruler can't be beat.

I'm always on the lookout for terrific new rulers. To get the accuracy I want, I look for rulers with lots of skinny lines that are easy to read. I want the back of the ruler to be slick enough that I can nudge it exactly into place but to have a little bit of a grip when I hold it down to cut. My current favorites are Creative Grids rulers. The black and white lines are easy to read, and the little etched dots on the back provide just enough grip. I'm also a fan of Omnigrid rulers. Their yellow markings are an issue for some folks, but they don't bother me. However, lacking grippies on the back, these do take a little more pressure to hold in place.

I do own a 6½″ × 24½″ ruler (just in case), but I don't know many quilters who can actually reach 24″ from their bodies. I don't use mine for basic cutting, but it's pretty handy for long bias strips.

Larger square rulers are wonderful for squaring up blocks and, of course, cutting larger chunks of fabric. I don't use my 20½″ square often, but it's a lifesaver when I need it.

Some folks suggest that we need to pick a brand and stick with it—that different brands are incompatible. But I'm of a mind that if it's accurate, it's accurate, whatever the brand. If two brands don't play well together, then one of them isn't accurate. Just saying.

Cutting Mats

It seems that no matter how big the mat, it's not quite big enough. I'm lucky to have a dedicated sewing space with a 3½-by-6-foot cutting table—which is wonderful when it isn't covered with stuff. In my early days I had a 24″ × 36″ mat that fit my kitchen counter. Go for the biggest mat your space allows.

The markings on mats don't matter much to me; I almost never use them for measuring. They just aren't accurate enough.

Wisps of fabric trapped in a mat's cutting lines are a sign that it's time for a new blade in the cutter. A dull blade will crush cotton lint right into the mat. Mats do wear out, and a scored and grooved mat can cause blades to chatter and skip.

Whatever size mat you use, store it flat. When my kitchen counter was tied up in food preparation, I used a bulldog clip to hang my little mat in the basement stairwell. Be especially wary of leaving a mat in a hot car; those curves can become permanent.

Turntable cutting mats are wonderful for quilters who do a lot of squaring up or paper piecing. It's pretty handy to be able to spin the mat instead of having to reposition the fabric.

Putting Your Tools to Work

Let's do some cutting up! We'll start with strategies for cutting accurate, tidy strips that are more or less on grain, with nary a wobble. From there we'll graduate to cutting strips into the building-block shapes for our quilts.

Folding Fabric for Cutting

As it comes off the bolt, quilting cotton is folded in half, to a width of 20″ or so. Some folks like to use a long ruler to cut their strips from the fabric with this one fold. I find it difficult to remain accurate for that length. Instead, I fold the fabric a second time, so that the center fold now lies along the selvages. For the first cut—the raw edge cleanup—I like to have the selvage edge on the top and nearest to me. (Lefties, or righties trying to cut with their nondominant hand, will have the selvage away.)

Smooth out any wrinkles, especially in the second fold. Don't try to align the raw edges. Sometimes, no matter how carefully the fabric has been cut (and even if it has been ripped on grain), there's waste in the raw edges. It's just the nature of the beast, and this is why we *always* buy extra fabric!

Cutting Strips

1. Start by cleaning up the ragged raw edge. Place your ruler on the fabric and slide it to the right (or the left, if you're a lefty) until it is near the raw edge. Check to be certain you'll be cutting away the edges on all 4 fabric layers.

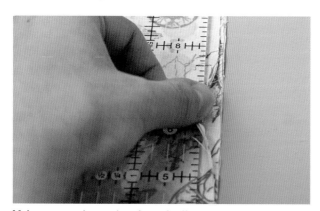

Make sure you're cutting through all the layers.

2. Make certain that the ruler is square on the fabric. Position a horizontal line on the ruler with the fold nearest to you. This is very important in order to avoid crooked strips. Check once more to make sure a horizontal line on the ruler is exactly on the fold. Cut away the ragged raw edge.

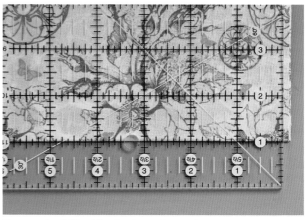

Line up the fold with a horizontal marking on the ruler.

3. Gently rotate the fabric so that the newly clean-cut edge is on your off-hand (nondominant) side. (Learn to cut with your off hand, and you won't need to rotate the fabric. Ahem.)

4. Place the ruler back on the fabric so that the strip measurement you want is aligned with the clean-cut edge and a horizontal line is even with a folded edge; using perpendicular reference lines will keep the cut straight. Make sure to have the measuring line fully on the fabric, not just touching the edge. Do this every time, and you'll never again be haunted by the dreaded scant ¼″ seam allowance—the tiny little width of that line gives you the extra threads you need for a great seam allowance.

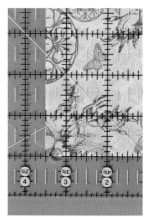

Position the measuring line on the cut.

THINKING ONCE: MARK YOUR SPOT

If a pattern calls for a bazillion strips cut to the same measurement, use a sticky note or highlighting tape to mark the measurement line on your ruler.

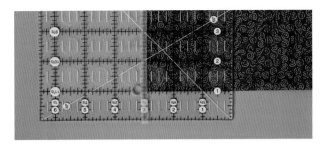

Tape the line on the ruler for easy repeated use.

Subcutting Shapes

Now let's cut our pretty strips into the shapes we need. Handle the strips carefully and as little as possible. The more we fool around with them before cutting the final shapes, the less accurate those shapes will be.

1. Open a strip so that it is only 2 layers thick, with a single fold. If you're cutting a bunch of the same shapes, you can stack strips. When I was younger, it was easy for me to cut through 8 layers and still end up with accurate pieces. Now I find that my limit is 6. Make the edges of the stacked strips as even as possible.

2. Trim off the selvage. By starting at the selvage edge and working toward the fold, you can often squeeze out more shapes. If nothing else, it will leave the largest possible scraps!

3. Place the measurement line for the shape fully on the fabric's edge (this is the trimmed selvage edge for the first cut). Align a horizontal measurement line along one raw edge—same principle as for cutting strips.

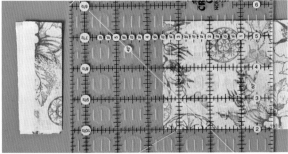

Align the strip with lines on the ruler, vertically and horizontally.

4. Make your cut. Before moving the ruler, gently pull the strip stack away from the cut shape, just a quarter-inch or so. Doing so will confirm that you've made a complete cut and will give you room to make more cuts as needed—as when a square is to be cut into triangles.

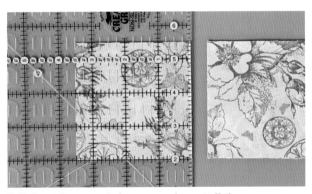

Pull the strips away to be sure you've cut all the way through.

THINKING ONCE: START BIG

Don't you hate it when a pattern directs you to cut an entire strip for just one square? I'd rather be left with yardage than with a stack of random strips.

To get the most out of your fabric, always start by cutting the widest strips first. Cut only the number of shapes required, and then cut the remainder of the strip down to the next largest strip size and start cutting those shapes. Often you'll end up with significant savings in fabric, and bigger scraps for your fabric stash.

squaring up

I look at squaring up as punishment for not sewing a block correctly in the first place. To me, it's time that could have been spent moving forward; it's also another opportunity to mess up. But others consider it worth the effort to be able to go to the next step with units that are exactly the right size.

The danger is that we'll just hack off fabric to make the block pretty. Seam allowances are necessary for sharp points and square squares. Intemperate trimming can leave us with dull stars and wonked-out four-patches. (Not that that's always a bad thing.)

Still, squaring up is written into lots of patterns, so let's take a look. A square ruler with a 45° line extending from a corner will make squaring up a lot easier. Newer 6½″ × 12½″ rulers also have this feature.

First, we measure. We can't start whacking stuff away until we know for sure that we have extra.

1. For a half-square triangle block (the samples here are from *Do Re Mi* on page 65), place the piece on the cutting mat with the seam angled up toward your dominant hand. Align the ruler's 45° line with the block's diagonal.

2. Shift the ruler until there's just the smallest amount of fabric showing toward your dominant-hand side. You're trimming away just crumbs here. Keeping the diagonal line on the seamline, trim the side and the top.

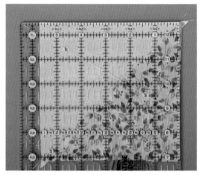

Trim the side and top to square up the block.

3. Now rotate the block so that the untrimmed edges are to the dominant-hand side and top.
Place the ruler on the square so the ruler's 45° line is on the seam and the measurement lines are on the previously trimmed edges. Trim away the excess.

Other blocks: As with half-square triangle blocks, first determine that, yea verily, there is enough extra fabric to trim away. Next figure out how to center the block under the ruler. Four-patches and Hourglass blocks are easy—the center is obvious. For other blocks, use the ruler's diagonal line to follow the corners across the squares. For blocks with points like those in *Mardi Gras* (page 89), make sure to leave enough seam allowance for the next seam. These seams are always measured *perpendicular* to the raw edge.

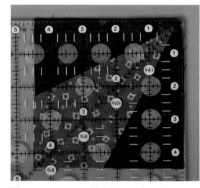

Measure perpendicular to the edge, not along the slant.

Diamonds and Parallelograms

Cutting a perfect diamond seems to be one of the hardest concepts in quilting, but diamonds are just pinched squares. To accurately cut diamonds, measure only through the middle, side to side at a right angle (perpendicular) to the edge, but never along an edge.

Parallelograms follow the same sequence, but they can have different widths and lengths.

1. To establish the angle on your strip, find the 45° line on the ruler. Align that with either the top or bottom of the strip, so that the ruler is slanting in a direction that's comfortable to cut. Trim away the selvage edge. You've created a 45° angle.

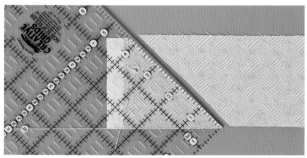

Cut off the selvage end at a 45° angle.

2. *Do not pick up or rotate the ruler!* Simply slide it forward, keeping that 45° line stuck firmly to the top or bottom edge of the strip. When your measurement line gets to the angled edge you've just cut, stop sliding. Don't rotate the ruler; just cut! You now have a perfect diamond.

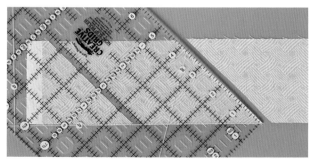

Place the measurement line on the cut edge.

Oversized Pieces

Sometimes even the biggest ruler just isn't big enough. But you can stretch your tools by folding the fabric.

For example, if you need a border strip 6½" × 39½", cut a strip 6½" × width of fabric (WOF). Open the folded strip so it has just one center fold. Half of 39½" is 19¾", so measure 19¾" from the fold and trim away the excess. *Voilà.*

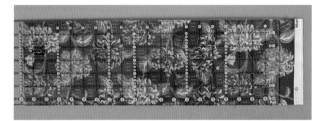

From the fold, measure half the desired strip size and cut.

For extra-large squares, start with a slightly oversized piece of fabric. Carefully fold it into quarters. Make sure the folded edges are under your ruler and the lines for *half* the desired final measurement are on the folds. Trim away the excess.

Fold the fabric into fourths, line up the folds, and trim.

You can also gang up rulers, using two rulers to add up to the required measurement. It can be tricky to keep the rulers square and tightly butted, but it does work in a pinch.

Wide Borders

My, how we love to put deliciously wide borders on our quilts! There's no better way to showcase that extravagantly large print fabric, the one that inspired the quilt in the first place. Cutting fabric with the straight grain will form a sturdy frame for the quilt top. To make sure the strips are perfectly on grain, I fall back on an old trick from my heirloom sewing days.

Tearing the fabric guarantees that borders will be on the straight grain, ensuring that the quilt will lie flat. To allow for the bruised edges that tearing often produces, add an inch or so to the desired width. Give the torn edges a crisp pressing and then carefully fold the border strips into manageable lengths. Use a ruler and rotary cutter to clean up the distorted edges. Check out Sneaky Trick: Measuring Your Borders (page 50).

Use a ruler and cutter to even out the torn strip edges.

Pieced Shapes

Sometimes our piecing process requires that we cut up parts that we've sewn together. Whether it involves strip piecing, squaring up, or one of the sneaky piecing strategies throughout this book, cutting through seams requires extra attention.

Strip sets

Strip piecing is a common strategy. Sewing strips together to cut into smaller units is thought of as a shortcut—I'm thinking, not so much. Really, we're going to be sewing and cutting exactly the same amount; we've just changed the order. I think it's so much easier to cut the basic shapes and sew them individually. It's hard to be accurate with long seams, and it's super easy to press strip sets out of shape.

That said, strip piecing is mighty nice for creating Lone Star or bargello quilts. We'll get to sewing and pressing

in the next two chapters, but let's continue our exploration of cutting techniques here.

When cutting strip sets, square the ruler on a *seamline*, not a raw edge. The seam is where the magic happens; the raw edges will disappear into seam allowances. Use two perpendicular lines to square the segments—one to measure from the cut edge and one on a seamline. For strips with multiple seams, choose one closest to the center of the strip.

Count on needing to resquare the measurement edge after a few cuts. This and squaring on the seam will give the truest cuts.

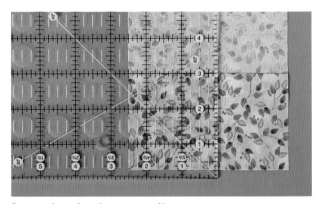

Square the ruler along a seamline.

Strip sets for Lone Star blocks

Cutting diamond strip sets follows the same idea as cutting straight strip sets, except that you cut on the diagonal. Be sure to measure through the strip, not along any raw edge, and keep as many ruler lines on as many seams as possible. Treat these strips with loving care—they are just begging to be stretched.

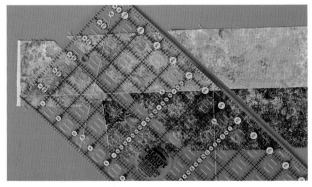

Cut the strip set on the diagonal to produce diamonds.

getting organized—it's in the bag

Nothing cheeses me more than having to look for things—especially having to look for the right hunk of fabric for the next step. Getting myself organized before I start sewing means I can just relax and sew.

When writing a piecing pattern, I assign a zip-top plastic bag (usually a quart or gallon size) to each step. As I cut the fabric, I zip the pieces into the appropriate bag. Now, as I sew, I have all the pieces I need—and only those pieces—for that step. Also, if I need to put the project away for a while, I can easily pick up where I left off.

For patterns that aren't written this way, organizing the pieces takes only a little workaround. Read the piecing directions before cutting the fabric. (Aren't we supposed to do that anyway?) Make a list of the parts needed for each step, one slip of paper per step. Put the lists into baggies and fill the bags as you cut the fabrics.

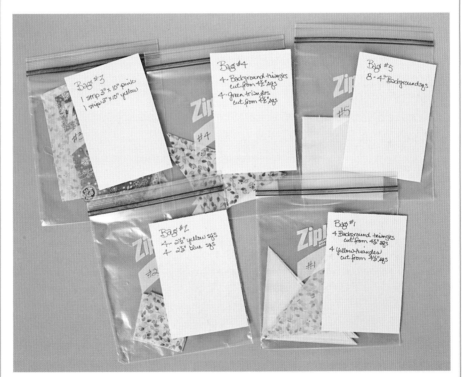

List what's needed for each bag, and then fill as you cut.

Sure, it can be like a little game of Concentration at first, matching cut pieces to your lists. But the time it takes at the start will come back to you in spades in time saved hunting down pieces or sewing the wrong ones together.

seams to me

Bring up the hallowed scant ¼″ seam allowance at a quilting function and see reactions ranging from haughty disregard to almost religious reverence. The reactions are all legitimate!

It's more or less true that for basic single-block quilts, pretty much any seam allowance will do. But the minute we start mixing blocks that have a different number of seams or angles, creative sewing can land us in a world of hurt. It's no fun at all trying to put together blocks that don't fit.

I figure that if we just learn to nail a good seam allowance, then the sky's the limit. Let's start with a look at the tools we need.

Tools of the Trade

Start with Thread

For piecing cotton quilting fabric, cotton thread is still the favorite. Cotton is toothy; it has a nappiness that clings to the fabric, which is especially handy when we're cutting our thread tails right to the edges. In contrast, polyester threads are slippery, allowing the last couple of stitches to pop loose. Having thread hold all the way to the edge makes it a lot easier to snuggle up seam allowances for cross seams.

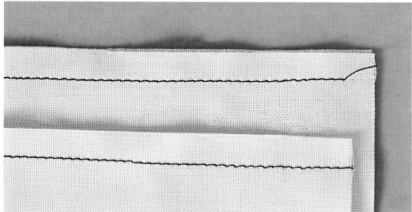

Cotton thread (bottom) grips the fabric all the way to the edge. Polyester thread (top) may pull free.

Thread needs to be strong enough to hold up to use but weak enough to fail under abuse. It's better for the stitching line to let go than for the fabric to tear. Broken seams can be repaired; fabric that has torn at the seamline will require a patch. Most polyester threads are simply too tough, and over time, they can actually cut the fabric at the seam.

Good thread, bad thread

Thread, like fabric, varies in quality. Price can be an indicator, but not always. Avoid threads that look fuzzy on the spool. Fuzzy threads can result in tons of lint in the sewing machine. Mercerized cotton threads have gone through a process to remove excess lint.

Thread weight

Alas, there is no real standardization for how thread is classified. Quilters gravitate to 50-weight cotton for piecing (the lower the number, the thicker the thread), but thread diameter can differ from one manufacturer to another. Some 50-weight cotton threads are three-ply (three strands twisted together); others are two-ply.

Finer threads, such as 60- or even 100-weight, are favored for appliqué, heirloom sewing, and machine quilting. They are also often used as bobbin threads in machine embroidery.

The color of the thread can also change its diameter. Darker dyes result in thicker threads. Can that make a difference? Well, yes and no. For most quilts, thread size won't matter a bit. But try to piece a tiny block, or one with lots of sharp points, and a fat thread can really get in the way.

My current favorite piecing thread is three-ply, 50-weight MasterPiece by Superior. Aurifil and Mettler are also excellent brands. For the majority of my piecing, I use soft white, medium gray, or dark gray, so I buy those in big cones. Of course, I have lots of other colors on spools.

Needles

Sewing machine needle size is usually given as two numbers—70/10, for example. The first number is the European size; the second, the American label. The larger the number, the thicker the needle.

Sharps, so called for their sharp points, are perfect for piercing quilting cottons. They easily plow through fabric, laying down a beautiful stitch. My go-to needle is a 70/10 sharp (also called microtex) by Schmetz. It gives me a sturdy but fine seamline.

Change needles frequently. Manufacturers recommend a new needle after about eight hours of stitching time. I might go a bit longer if I'm piecing (when stitches will be hidden in the seams), but I will change a lot sooner if I am quilting with decorative threads.

Sewing Machines

You don't need a top-of-the-line sewing machine to make excellent quilts. (However, if you'd like justification for one, I can help you with that.) What you *do* need is a machine that will sew a nice, straight seam without a battle. Keep in mind that sewing machine stores have entry-level machines at the same prices as the big-box stores. A used machine from a reputable dealer is an excellent way to get more features at a bargain price.

Each of the many brands of machines has its own personality. It's hard to go wrong when buying from dealerships; they have an investment in offering machines that perform well. Most important, the dealership should be a place where you feel comfortable asking questions and seeking help. A good dealership will offer classes on using its machines. All those fancy functions are no good at all if you don't know how to apply them.

Take along your favorite type of fabric to test-drive machines. Make a list of features you'd like. The following are some of my favorites.

¼˝ **foot that really is** ¼˝. A sewing machine presser foot that will help you get a correct-sized seam allowance is the best tool you can have. I especially like having markings ¼˝ in front and back of the needle, which is handy when attaching binding and insetting seams. It's terrific if ¼˝ is also marked on both sides of the foot.

I'm not a big fan of patchwork feet with blades or guides on the side. I've seen students pack a ½˝ seam allowance into that space. The blade can make it harder to see whether the fabric is feeding properly. That said, if it works for you, then it's the right foot for the job!

Walking or even-feed foot. Originally designed for matching plaids or sewing bulky, stretchy fabrics, the walking foot (also called an even-feed or dual-feed foot) is loved for straight-line machine quilting and applying bindings. Although generic feet are available to fit almost any machine, a walking foot designed specifically for your machine will always work best. Some machines come with an integrated dual-feed function.

Feed dogs that feed straight. You shouldn't have to fight your machine to get a straight seam. Fabric should feed under the foot with only gentle guidance. Feed dogs can droop over time (gravity gets us all, eventually). If it feels like the foot is skating around on the fabric or not feeding properly, it's time to see the repair guy.

Single-stitch throat plate. All zigzag machines come with a throat plate (that silver thing that surrounds the feed dogs) with an oval opening that allows the needle to swing from side to side to make the zigzag stitch. It also allows fabric to ride up and down on the needle. Called "flagging," the up part isn't so bad, but it's frustrating when the needle drags fabric down into the bobbin area to be chewed to bits.

A single-stitch (straight-stitch) throat plate has only a small circle for the needle to pass through. There's no extra room for the fabric to be pulled down, which lets us sew even the pointiest seams with no worries.

Needle up/needle down function. Being able to program the machine to stop with the needle down in the fabric is a great feature. Stopping with the needle down pins the fabric in place while you pause to get things adjusted. The next stitch will fall exactly in line.

Hands-free function. It's really handy to be able to drop or lift the needle without having to reach for the hand wheel. On several brands, a simple tap of the power pedal will control the needle position. Others have a button within easy reach.

Likewise, being able to lift the presser foot hands-free is fantastic for making fine adjustments to fabrics. Some brands have knee-activated levers; others have electronic options for lifting the foot when you let up on the gas.

Easy tension adjustment. I shy away from anything that says it's automatic; it tends to mean "hard to adjust." I use all sorts of threads for quilting, from super-fine silk to bulky perle cotton. If I can't get it through the eye of a needle, I'll wrap it on a bobbin. Different thread weights often require adjusting the tension.

Check your manual to make sure you are winding the bobbin and threading the machine properly. It really does make a difference.

THINKING ONCE: AN OUNCE OF PREVENTION

A machine that is used regularly needs a "well-baby visit" to the repair shop at least once a year to be cleaned, oiled, and adjusted. If the machine has been purchased from a dealer, this tune-up often is included in the purchase price.

Check the manual for your machine's routine maintenance needs. At the very least, regularly remove the throat plate to clean out the lint. Lint can trap moisture and lead to rusted parts. It soaks up machine oil, leaving parts grinding themselves to dust. It can even keep the feed dogs from operating properly.

Finding That ¼″

Take a moment to examine your machine. Sure, you may have a special piecing foot installed, but you still need to understand where the fabric should line up.

1. Position a ruler under the foot as if it were a piece of fabric needing a ¼″ seam. Lower the foot to hold the ruler in place. Adjust the ruler so that one of its horizontal lines is even with the front edge of the throat plate.

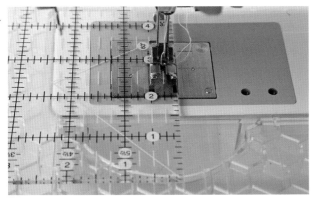

Square the ruler over the throat plate.

2. Gently, using the hand wheel, lower the needle so that it just touches the ruler. For a perfect ¼″ seam allowance, the *left* side of the needle should touch the *right* side of the line. The entire needle should fall within the ¼″ seam allowance. If necessary, adjust the ruler. Notice where its edge is in comparison to the side of the foot.

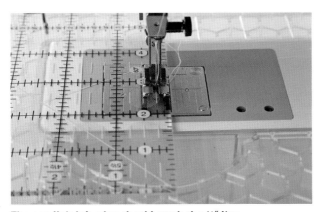

The needle's left edge should touch the ¼″ line.

3. Look for a marking line on the machine near the front of the presser foot; on my machine, there's a little hash mark in front of the right feed dog. This is where to watch as you feed in fabric. If you watch at the side of the foot by the needle, it will be too late to do any adjusting.

Using a Landing Strip

Sometimes it's a real challenge to feed in fabric as straight as we'd like. We can help by giving ourselves a guideline in front of the foot. I think of it as a landing strip. It's kind of like the difference between landing a helicopter and landing a jumbo jet. Trying to align fabric at the needle doesn't give us time to make corrections—it's like a helicopter dropping out of the sky. To land a jumbo jet, the pilot must get the plane lined up miles away.

A landing strip can help keep fabric moving smoothly. Some folks like to use a stack of sticky notes or a magnetic seam guide. These work great, unless we let the fabric curl up against them. They are also in the way for sewing larger pieces. I prefer to use a piece of ¼″ quilter's tape as my guide. It's never in the way.

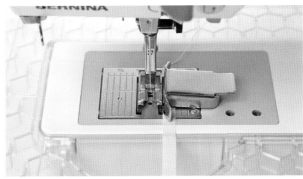

Quilter's tape makes a convenient fabric guide.

What about Stitch Length?

When I bought my first electronic machine, the default stitch length was so short, I thought I'd die of old age before finishing my first seam. Turns out I'd practically been basting with my old machine.

The ideal stitch length is 12 to 14 stitches per inch. Too long, and the stitches will break and pull out too easily; too short, and they can damage the fabric and be hard to remove should we need to rip the seam.

A Word about Marking Tools

Yikes.

That's my word about marking tools. Seriously though, we need to understand how marking devices will interact with our fabric before we go scribbling all over our quilts.

After I had an air-soluble pen permanently discolor a project, such markers are now permanently off my list. Although the markings originally disappeared as promised, over time, brown lines took their place, despite frequent and careful washing.

When using water-soluble markers, be sure to test them using the washing method you'll use on the finished quilt. Some soaps and detergents actually can make the marks permanent. The heat of an iron also can set marks. Read the packaging to be sure.

I like to use either a graphite pencil (a cheap mechanical one works for me) or, for dark fabrics, a fabric pencil with white ceramic lead. These don't bleed, and they brush away easily. For permanent marks, stick with pens designed for fabric, such as Pigma or Fabrico. Although Sharpies can make a bold line, over time the marks can develop an ugly yellow halo.

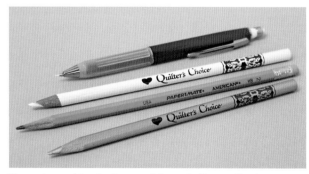

My go-to marking tools are white and silver quilter's pencils, an ordinary writing pencil (super sharp), and a white mechanical pencil.

Piecing

Now that our machines are set up and the parts for our quilts have been wonderfully cut, let's get sewing.

 THINKING ONCE: THE TEMPLATE LAYER

Even if you've sorted your pieces into bags, you'll start out with a jumble of parts. A quick read-through of project directions will tell you what you need first. Find those pieces and stash the rest out of the way. Arrange a layer of pieces in their block configuration and stack the rest on top. (Make sure any sneaky tone-on-tone fabrics are right side up.) Now you can sew without worries.

Arrange stacked pieces in their block positions.

Assembly-Line Sewing

Anytime we're stitching one fabric pair on the heels of another, we're doing assembly-line sewing—also known as chain piecing. The goal is to have just one stitch in the air between the pairs. To do this, we butt the next set right up against the fabric under the presser foot; the pieces will naturally separate just enough as they advance.

It's not just about saving thread. Assembly-line sewing is a powerful organizing tool. Start by laying out all the parts of the block, feeding in each of the fabric pairs in order. Then the stitching line can serve as pins, holding everything in place until the final seam is sewn.

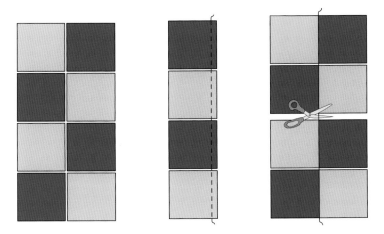

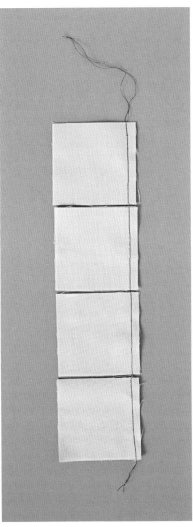

Sew multiple fabric pairs with a single line of stitching.

The threads *within* a block are never snipped, and I wait until after pressing to snip the seams between the blocks. Keeping them all strung together means I'm less likely to lose a piece along the way. Who wants to spend time looking for a chunk of a quilt, only to discover that you've worn it to the grocery store stuck to the back of your thigh?

Assembly-line sewing can improve our seam allowance also. We tend to start seams a little on the generous side, and then we wander off a bit, ending with a slightly smaller seam allowance. With assembly-line sewing, we may still have that chubby seam allowance at the start of a line of piecing and that skinny one at the end, but sewing from one pair directly onto the next helps us keep a more consistent seam allowance.

check sum

A "check sum" is a number used to quickly confirm that our math has been performed properly. We can use the same concept in piecing.

We often find ourselves sewing a pieced unit to a simple cut shape. I know that the more actions I perform on fabric, the less accurate the final piece is going to be. In other words, a plain cut square will be more accurate than a pieced square. So any time we're joining a cut unit to a pieced unit, it's an opportunity to check how we're doing with that pesky seam allowance.

If the pieced unit is bigger than the cut unit, the seam is too narrow. If the pieced unit is smaller, then the seam allowance is too big. Instead of pulling and easing to fit, take a few moments to consider what adjustments are needed.

I think of every seam that I sew as practice for the next one. I'll admit that I feel a little smug satisfaction when my piecing measures up. But that feeling is usually short lived, of course, because new opportunities for humility are always just around the corner.

Compare the pieced unit to the cut shape.

Beth says:

"Anything worth doing is worth doing badly for as long as it takes."

Why are there gathers?

Sometimes when we're sewing long strips together, we end up with shirring or gathering. This can be caused by tension that's out of whack. The seam should lie prettily on the fabric—both on top and on bottom—with nice stitch definition on both sides.

When a thread is too tight, it will look pulled, with the opposite thread forming loops over it. Loosen the tension on the thread that looks pulled. (Loosen = lower number.) Move half an increment at a time.

Sometimes strips are ruffled because we've manhandled them through the machine. Never pull fabric out from behind the foot—let the feed dogs do the work. If fabric doesn't advance well on its own, it's time for a trip to the sewing machine doctor.

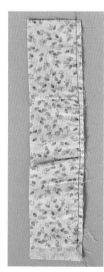

Incorrect tension can make the fabric pucker.

Nesting strip-pieced seams

To create beautiful intersections, seams need to be nicely mated. Layer pieced strips (or strip sets) right sides together and rub your fingers over the seams— as if you were making a clay snake. You can feel when seams are nested close together because the seam allowances will be the same height. Caress the seams until they're snuggled together the length of the strips. Now the segments will be paired up and ready to sew as you cut them.

Use your fingers to feel whether seams are aligned.

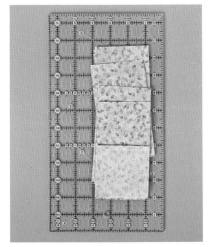
A ruler does double duty by keeping segments in order.

Pinning

I think pins often cause more problems than they solve. Shoving a pin into a seamline just pushes the seam apart. And if we place the pin in front of a seam, then when we pull it out to sew (because we never, ever sew over pins, right?), that little bubble of fabric that often rides in front of the presser foot will push the seams apart.

Instead, I'm a touchy-feely sort of piecer. My forefinger rides the intersection right up to the needle. If I feel the seams are pulling apart or trying to overlap, I can ease the fabrics into position. Most of the time, just the pressure of my finger is enough to hold the seams in the right place. Give it a try.

If pinning *is* necessary, place the pin on the far side of the intersecting seam allowance. That will keep the fabric from shifting until the intersection is nailed down.

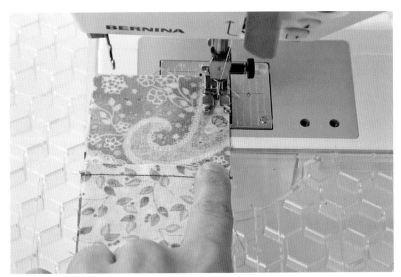
A finger on the fabric can take the place of pinning.

Sewing Half-Square Triangles

It's a simple fact of geometry: A seam allowance discrepancy that we might be able to live with on straight seams will give us heartache on angled seams. And the steeper the angle, the more the error is magnified.

Also, bias edges are the bogeymen of the quilting universe, scarily easy to stretch out of shape. We need to be able to rely on the feed dogs to gently advance both layers of fabric, at the same rate, so that there's no need to manhandle the fabric. The more we have to push, pull, or cajole our fabric through the machine, the less likely we are to end up with pretty bias seams.

outwitting the feed dogs

sneaky piecing tricks

One challenge when piecing triangles is those darned hungry feed dogs. Trying to start a seam allowance near the triangle points can result in the fabric being pulled down into the machine to be chewed to bits. Here are three of my favorite sneaky tricks for keeping points intact.

Trick 1: The single-stitch throat plate.

A single-stitch throat plate will pretty much solve this problem, but not all machines have one to purchase. If necessary, you can make your own: Trim a tiny piece of template plastic to fit between the feed dogs, and then punch a small hole in it for the needle. Use sandpaper to remove any rough edges on the hole. Tape this bit of plastic over the oval opening of the machine's throat plate, and there you go. (Remove it before changing over to zigzag, or it will be time to make a new one.)

A homemade throat plate can keep the feed dogs at bay.

Trick 2: Thread bunnies. These are just small squares of fabric used to support the points of triangles as you begin sewing. Usually they consist of a couple layers of fabric scraps, maybe an inch or so square. You start by sewing onto the bunny and then continue stitching onto the triangles. Assembly-line sewing triangles lets the adjoining pairs support the overlapping points.

Trick 3: Disappearing bunnies. For piecing super-sharp points, use a small piece of water-soluble paper to support the fabric. The paper will dissolve in the wash, so you won't ever have to pull it away from the piecing. Leaving the paper in place as seams are pressed supports the seams right out to the last thread of the point. The paper can stay in place as the skinny points are sewn; any excess can be trimmed away with the dog ears.

Thread bunnies support the free ends of the triangles.

Water-soluble thread bunnies disappear in the wash.

double-duty as thread bunnies

I'm nothing if not frugal, and water-soluble paper isn't free. I make mine do double-duty, first as quilting guides and then as disappearing thread bunnies.

I hate marking my quilts because every line I draw is a line I have to worry about removing. Instead, I print or trace my quilting design onto water-soluble paper. I stack up a few layers of the paper and staple them together. Using a honking big needle (such as a 110/18) without thread, I follow the lines of the design and free-motion stitch through the stack, perforating the layers.

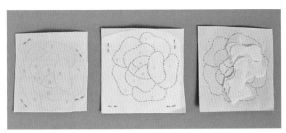

Use the paper as a quilting guide, and then recycle it as thread bunnies.

I pin one of the sheets on the quilt top and free-motion quilt along the perforations. When I remove the paper, I don't have to worry about trying to tease out every last little bit; it will disappear with the first washing!

Drawing or cutting?

Some quilters prefer to draw diagonal guidelines on squares instead of going ahead and cutting triangles. Indeed, sewing those bias edges before cutting them can minimize stretching. Beware, though—it's easy to be lulled into sloppiness. We still need to sew accurately! I'd rather cut my triangles and be done with it than spend the extra time drawing lines.

Connecting Corners

So-called connecting corners are a super power that can be used for both good and evil.

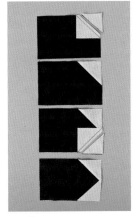

Small squares are sewn in the corners, trimmed, and turned.

Sewing on a line across a corner helps us sew blocks that would be a challenge otherwise. This technique is used for the little stars in *Night Skies* (page 71). Align small squares of fabric with the corners of larger hunks, right sides together. Stitch on the diagonal between the outer points of the little square and then trim away the corner, leaving a ¼″ seam allowance. Usually the seam is pressed toward the corner, but that depends on the final design.

Some quilters leave the extra corner fabric in place as a fail-safe in case their stitching is off. I prefer to trim it away so that my piecing all has the same thickness.

The "evil" comes when we end up trimming away a ton of fabric. When the connecting corners technique is used to create Flying Geese, for example, there's so much waste, we could make another quilt! How silly, especially when there are easier ways to sew geese with no biases and no waste—but that's in the next chapter.

THINKING ONCE: SEWING UNITS INTO BLOCKS

Sewing units into blocks is where assembly-line sewing really shines. I've used the Homecoming block from *Do Re Mi* (page 65) in these examples.

There's so much that could go wrong with this block. The half-square triangles need to be turned just so, as do the four-patches. If we have to keep stopping to think which pieces to sew next, we court disaster. Instead, we can think once and enjoy our sewing time.

1. Set out a layer of block components as a template. Stack the remaining units on top.

Lay out the pieces the way that they'll be sewn together.

2. Assembly-line sew the units, starting with the top pair and then the next pair. Remember that the goal is just a single stitch in the space between the units.

3. Continue sewing the top pair and then the bottom pair until all the units are sewn. Don't cut those threads! Threads are cut *between* the blocks, but only after they've been pressed. Peek ahead to see how flip-flop pressing (page 40) is the coolest trick ever for pressing these blocks.

Stitch together with assembly-line sewing.

Positioning Triangles

When aligning a square and a triangle, use their right-angle corners to position them. The points of the triangle should extend past the edges of the square. These are called "dog ears."

Your ¼˝ seam allowance should fall exactly where the cut bias edge of the triangle intersects the square's raw edge. Always trim away dog ears after sewing and pressing.

The triangle's long side meets the edge of the square at the seamline.

sashing as you go

sneaky piecing tricks

A sashed quilt is one in which the basic blocks are separated by another element. Think of it as an old-fashioned multipaned window—indeed, that's where the term originated. Sashing can be as simple as plain fabric, as in *Oopsie Daisies* (page 77), or it can be pieced, as in *Do Re Mi* (page 65).

A common method is to sew wide rows of blocks separated by sashing strips, followed by narrow rows of sashing strips alternated with corner-stone pieces. These rows are then sewn together. But I've always found it difficult to manage rows that are so different in size. I prefer to sew on the sashing as each block is completed, allowing me to sew similar-size rows together. I start by choosing two adjacent block sides to which I will sew the sashing first—often the right edge and the bottom.

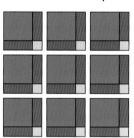

Start along adjacent sides—in this case, the right and bottom edges.

The seams are usually pressed toward the sashing strips—unless, of course, the strips are made of background fabric (because we usually press away from the background fabric). The blocks along the remaining two quilt edges will need additional sashing strips. When the blocks are all sashed, it's a simple task to sew these slightly larger blocks together.

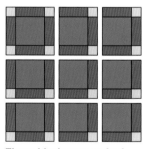

These blocks are sashed and ready to be sewn together in rows.

Taking on Challenging Blocks

Some traditional blocks have gotten a bad rap. Labeled "challenging," most of these are not really as difficult as might be suggested—especially when there are sneaky piecing tricks to apply.

Sewing Perfect Points

Lining up basic right-angle seams is pretty straightforward. The training wheels come off, though, when we're trying to get angled seams aligned for perfect points—as in the Lone Star block in *Sur la Table* (page 83).

The secret lies in learning how to offset the seamlines. Angled seams need to cross at the seamline, *not* at the edges of the pieces.

Seam allowances are *always* measured perpendicularly from the raw edge. However, it can be a pain to use a ruler to measure each intersection. So here's one of my very favorite sneaky piecing tricks.

---

thumbing it

sneaky piecing tricks

Designed for hand quilters to use for marking grid lines, ¼˝ masking tape is equally useful for measuring a seam allowance offset. Here's how:

1. Fold a piece of ¼˝ tape over the end of your nondominant thumb. You now have a handy (pun intended) measuring device that lets you put your seams in place!

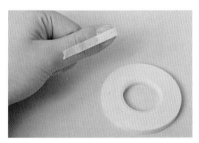

Quilter's tape on your thumb is a measuring device that's always close at hand.

2. Hold the fabric units to be joined with right sides together. Keep the fold of the tape on the end of your thumb perpendicular to the raw edge. Use the tape to measure ¼˝ from the edge to the angled seam on the top unit; insert a pin into that layer at that point.

Use a pin to mark where the tape meets the angled seam.

3. Where your measuring tape meets the seam on the second unit (its right side toward you), stick the same pin through at that spot.

Poke the pin through where the tape meets the seam on the second layer.

4. What you *don't* want to do now is turn the pin up to keep it in place because that would shift the layers out of position. Instead, keeping the marking pin vertical, insert another pin after the seamline to hold the layers in position. The marking pin can now be removed.

Keeping the first pin vertical, use another pin to hold the units together.

Nailing these angled seams takes practice. As with all things, the more you do, the better you get, until you're able to eyeball where seams should cross.

acing inset seams

To many quilters, Eight-Point Star blocks are just plain showing off. The bias-edge diamond shapes and inset background pieces can be pretty scary. But just think of these blocks as a really sexy bunch of partial seams.

To begin, you need to know where to start and end the seams—the spots where they intersect.

Marking Your Spots

A template makes it easy to mark your spots. If you're making only a couple of blocks, a paper or card stock template will do just fine. For a quilt's worth of stars, use template plastic.

1. Cut a diamond of template material the size called for in your pattern. Mark the ¼″ seamlines on the template. An ultrafine Sharpie works great for this. Be as precise as possible.

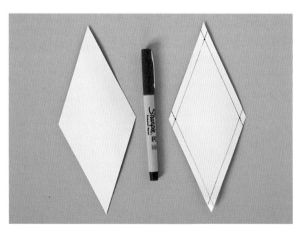

Mark the seamlines on the template.

2. The starting and stopping points for your seams are where the seamlines cross. A ⅟₁₆″-circle hand punch (your local quilt shop can order you one for less than $10) makes the perfect hole in the template for marking these spots. Mark each one on the wrong side of the fabric. The marks will be right on the stitching lines, so don't use a marker that might bleed.

3. Make a right-angle template for the block's background squares and triangles. Cut a square that's 2″ or so, mark the ¼″ seam allowance on 2 adjacent sides, and punch a hole where they cross. Now mark—on the wrong side—the right angle on the triangles and one corner on each square.

Mark the seamlines on 2 sides.

Sewing Order

Whether diamonds are simply cut from fabric (like the ones shown) or pieced (as in *Sur la Table*, page 83), the sewing order is the same.

1. Sew the diamonds into pairs. Make sure to have the same fabric on top for each pair, or you'll end up with a mirror image. Start at one marked dot and stitch to the other dot. (Some folks like to back-stitch at the beginning and end. I don't, since I sometimes need to pick out a stitch or two to get the seam just right.) Hold off on pressing for now.

Sew diamond pairs together between the dots.

2. Set the background triangles into the diamond pairs. Holding a pair with the seam to the left, gently fold up the top diamond to expose the beginning of the seam. With right sides together, line up the dot on the triangle with the seam end. Stitch, starting at the triangle dot and sewing all the way off the edge of the diamond pair.

When setting in seams, always start at the end of a previously stitched seam. Any time you sew *toward* a fixed point (such as a seam), you're just begging for pleats and puckers.

3. Flip the piece over and align the second diamond with the other side of the triangle. Begin sewing where the diamond-pair seam ends and stitch off the end of the fabric.

Sew one side of the triangle, then the other.

4. Press the seams toward the diamonds, starting with the diamond on the left.

5. Sew the diamond pairs into pairs. Sew from dot to dot, right sides of the diamonds together, folding seam allowances out of the way.

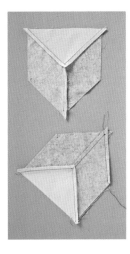

6. Set in the corner squares, starting at the end of the diamond-pair seam and sewing off the edge of the square, which should line up with the long edge of the setting triangles.

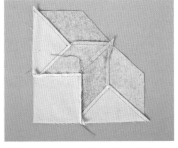

Add corner squares to the stitched-together diamond pairs.

7. Sew together the block halves. Start at the center and sew outward, taking care not to sew over the pointy seam allowances in the middle. Press the diamond seams so they spiral around the block. With your thumb, mash down those free points, giving them a good twist. They should fan out into a lovely, flat circle. Finish by insetting the final 2 corner squares.

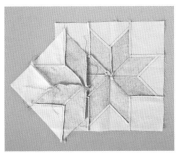

Sew together the block halves, working out from the center.

Sewing Partial Seams

Some blocks appear impossible to sew, as if there's just nowhere to start. The secret lies in sewing only a portion of the first seam, stopping short of the end of the fabric, and leaving enough room to finish later. There are four such blocks in *Sur la Table* (page 83).

1. Align the block's center square with the first rectangle, right sides together. Stitch, stopping about 1˝ from the edge of the square. Lightly press this seam before sewing the next rectangle in place; a hard crease can make it harder to finish later.

Stop short of the end on the first seam; then continue the sequence.

2. The next seam will span the end of the rectangle and the square, as will the next and the next; press each seam as you go. Once you've made it all the way around the center square, go back to finish that first seam. Easy peasy.

Unsewing

Where there is sewing, there must sometimes be unsewing. Also known as frog stitching or frogging because we need to rip it, rip it, rip it (hey, I didn't make this up), taking out stitches is just a part of our quilting life.

To avoid damaging fabric, invest in a good seam ripper. It needs to be sharp, with a blade fine enough to wiggle under stitches. To remove a seam, use the ripper to cut every third or fourth stitch on the needle side of the fabric. Pull the bobbin thread to pop out the remaining stitches. It's easier to pull free the bobbin thread than the needle thread, which has been poked down into the fabric. Use a lint roller to clean up the thread bits; sewing over them will make them harder to remove later.

Use a seam ripper to cut stitches; tidy up with a lint roller.

After a seam has been sewn and unsewn more than twice, the fabric has been pretty much reduced to rubble. Let's face it—if we haven't gotten it right in two passes, we have more to learn before we can succeed. Put it aside and move on to the next block for a time. Instead of worrying those poor hunks of fabric to death, practice on scrap fabric. Better yet, take a break, walk the dog, eat some chocolate—anything to soothe the frustration.

Consider every quilt as practice for the next one. I always try to do my best, but I gave up "perfect" many years ago. Trying to be perfect has a way of sucking all the joy out of life. I know; I'm a recovering perfectionist.

Beth says:

"Don't sacrifice the good on the altar of the perfect."

pressing matters

All our careful cutting and vigilant sewing can be dashed to bits on the rocks of wicked ironing. We yank fabric this way and that. We mash down whatever sticks up. And heaven forbid we should get out of our seats and actually go to an ironing board.

I'll admit it: I'm a pressing fanatic. So many times I've seen quilters do lovely, precise work, only to iron everything out of kilter. We attack our fabric as if it must be beat into submission.

Tools of the Trade

The Perfect Iron

I have to say, so far my perfect iron doesn't exist. That doesn't keep me from buying and trying every new innovation that comes along. Just as no one brand of sewing machine is right for every quilter, different irons will appeal to different quilters. That said, here are some features I look for in an iron.

Hot, hot, hot! I keep my iron set on scorch. Some newer irons have limits on how hot they can get. In an attempt to keep us from burning ourselves, and bringing a lawsuit, some manufacturers produce irons that just don't get really hot. I wonder if we can sue for that?

Always on. The automatic shutoff feature is nice if you tend to iron your shirts just before dashing away to work and forget to turn off the iron. But for piecing, automatic shutoff basically means "always cold." If this function can't be disabled, the iron is automatically off my list.

Sharp nose. The nose of the iron is used to nudge seams to one side. When the nose is rounded or blunt or thick, it's hard to finesse seams into place. It's extra nice if the soleplate is thin, with a nice button groove, which gives you lots of control.

Good weight, good balance. The lighter the iron, the harder we need to press down for crisp seams. On the other hand, an iron that's too heavy will tire us out faster and be harder to control. A well-balanced iron should be relatively heavy but still be easy to maneuver.

Easy to clean. An easy-to-clean soleplate is especially important for folks who use fusible webbing in their quilts. No matter how careful we are, the webbing is bound to get on the iron. I use lots of Magic Sizing starch (more on that in a minute), and it does tend to build up after a year or two.

Steam?

I'm not a fan of using steam when pressing for piecing. In addition to shrinking the fabric, a good head of steam makes it tough to get our fingers close to the soleplate to manage pressing. Steam also makes the fabric limp and more easily distorted.

For those who do use steam (and it's mighty nice for pressing tablecloths), it's important that the iron generates a good amount of steam and that it doesn't spit and leak.

Travel irons, cordless, and other gimmicks

Irons of various sizes for various purposes

A full-size iron, a garment steamer, and a travel iron cover a range of pressing needs.

When traveling to quilt conferences, check the fine print for the rules on irons. Anything that makes heat draws lots of power. We can plug in a roomful of sewing machines with no problems, but a couple of irons can blow the circuits for half of a conference center. Little travel irons are great for casual pressing at retreats, though their small size and light weight will make us work harder.

I generally don't run around the room ironing stuff, so the whole cordless bit is pretty much lost on me. But for an art quilter who fuses great swaths of fabric, a cordless iron could be a godsend.

For a while, I tried an iron that sits soleplate down and that hops up when you let go. It was nice not to have to twist my wrist to set the iron on its heel, but the nose was too blunt, and the iron didn't feel balanced. I also tried an inexpensive model recommended for its high temperature, but it was so lightweight that it made pressing a chore.

Even though I've had dalliances with sexier irons, I keep going back to my old Rowenta Professional. I've had it for years. It's been knocked to the floor repeatedly. It's been left on for hours and hours. It's absolutely perfect, as long as I don't put water in it (it leaks like nobody's business). I'm good with that.

THINKING ONCE: EXTENSION CORDS

When it comes to electricity, the farther we get from the outlet, the more power we lose along the way. If we plug our big old iron into a wimpy little extension cord, it will make lots of heat along the way, but our iron won't get as hot. Quilt guilds often need to use extension cords at their workshops. Invest in heavy-duty cords to carry the power from the wall, and check with the building manager to take advantage of outlets on different circuits.

Pressing Stations

For most of us, a good old ironing board is just what we need for pressing our piecing. I'm happy to have a slightly wider, European-style board. Rectangular covers for generic boards add more pressing space. But what's most important is the ability to adjust the height of the board.

Stand in front of the board with the iron flat on its soleplate. Ideally, the top of the iron handle should be about elbow height. You should be able to lift the iron an inch or so without having to raise your shoulder.

When it comes to covers, I'm a canvas sort of girl. I like the toothiness of canvas. The shiny, silicone covers let my pieces slide all over the place, making it more like a game of tag than a pressing session. Canvas, on the other hand, grips the pieces, letting me micromanage the shapes.

I also like a little bit of padding under the cover. Usually there's enough just from putting a new cover over the old one. A little padding lets the seam allowances sink in a little, giving a good, sharp press. A hard surface magnifies all the different depths of the piecing.

Our Quilting Nests

We love to get ourselves set up into a little hive of productivity, with our cutting, sewing, and pressing all within easy reach of our rolling chairs. Although this is great for short-term setups at retreats, it's not terrific for our everyday quilting.

It's human nature that we don't take the trouble to fully turn toward our pressing setup. But being even slightly turned away from our work means we'll be pressing arcs into our piecing. If, instead, we face the pressing station squarely, we'll be able press our pieces straight and true.

aerobic pressing

sneaky piecing tricks

It's important for our health to get up and go to the ironing board. A jaunt to the ironing surface every few minutes will help circulate the blood out of our legs, minimizing the chances of blood clots. While some quilters have health issues that necessitate sitting down, for most of us, a trip to the iron is as good for the body as it is for the quilt.

Starch versus Sizing

Softening fabric by washing it makes a lot of sense for hand piecers. But for machine piecing, fabric with body makes sewing much easier. Spray sizing (or a starch alternative) is the answer. Magic Sizing is my favorite brand; it doesn't build up, and there's no flaking. I use it on every trip to the ironing board.

After pressing your fabric into the desired position, let it cool just a bit before spraying on the sizing. Fabric that's too hot will just sizzle the sizing away. No need to saturate the fabric; just a light pass at each pressing will keep it nice and crisp for the next step.

Spray sizing is *not* the same as spray starch. Sizing is a synthetic product; starch is food for critters. Silverfish, especially, love to snack on starch. The problem is that they end up snacking on the fabric as well.

Sizing or spray starch alternative can make fabric easier to handle.

Some folks like to make their own spray starch, diluting the liquid starch found in the laundry aisle and putting it in a spray bottle. I find this concoction entirely too wet. I've seen students wildly distort their pieces by using "home brew" starch. The wet pieces are easily ironed out of shape and then frozen that way by the starch.

Let's Start Pressing!

Let's get down to the nitty-gritty of excellent pressing techniques. Notice that it's called pressing, not ironing. Ironing is for shirts; pressing is for piecing. If the iron is moving, there should be no pressure on the fabric. The iron hovers just above the fabric when in motion and is then pressed down to set the fabric in place.

Before we can apply iron to fabric, we have to decide how we will press the seam. Pressing the seam allowances to one side is standard in traditional piecing—the seams are sturdy and, when carefully planned, can be snuggled together for showy intersections. How seams are pressed can influence the final quilting design, since the "ditch"—as in "stitch in-the-ditch"—falls on the lower side of the seam, or the fabric the seam has been pressed away from.

The Number One Rule of Pressing

I bet you're already muttering, "Ho hum, I know this. We always press toward the dark." But I'm here to tell you that this is one of those darned lies of quilting!

Instead, we always press *away from the background fabric.*

Everyone say it with me. How do we press?

Away from the background fabric.

To make our quilts truly spectacular, we need to be thinking about our plan for quilting while we're sewing the pieces together. For me, deciding which way a seam is to be pressed is all about the ditch.

The fabric toward which a seam is pressed will be lifted forward visually. The ditch will fall next to that fold, on the other fabric. When we quilt in that ditch, our foreground fabric becomes even more pronounced. Every time we sew a seam, we have an opportunity to decide which fabric plays the main character and which becomes the supporting cast.

Let's look at *Night Skies* (page 71)—the one with the lovely, bright stars on that deep, dark background. If we were to follow the old rule and press all the seams toward the dark, the star blocks would visually retreat. Should we then want to stitch in-the-ditch around the stars, the quilting line would press the stars into the background instead of showcasing them.

But when we press the seams *away from the background* (in this case, toward the yellow star fabrics), we lift the stars, putting them visually in front of the background.

Let's go one more step and look at the yellow stars with the red centers. These seams don't involve the background fabric, so we don't have the easy answer of pressing away from the background. If we press the seams toward the red fabric, the little star will look like it's floating in front of the larger yellow star. If we press the seams toward the yellow, the little red star will look like it's shining through a hole in the yellow star. Which is right? We get to decide!

Every fabric pair has a background fabric, even if it's not *the* background fabric of the quilt. By choosing which fabric will play second fiddle, we can make it the background fabric for that pair.

Herein lies my chief complaint with paper piecing. This flip-and-sew method—stitching through printed paper foundations—doesn't let us control the direction in which our seam allowances are pressed. In fact, we often start with the focal area in the center and build out from there, pushing the center design deeper and deeper into the background.

Start with a four-patch

For illustration, let's strip-piece a simple little four-patch. In the example, the dark fabric is the background fabric.

1. Place the pieced strips on your pressing surface with the fabric toward which the seam will be pressed on top and the seam away from you.

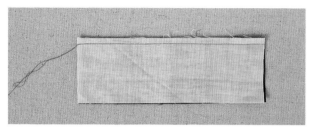

Lay out the strip unit with the seam away from you.

THINKING ONCE: THE B RULE

Getting seam allowances pressed in the right directions will be easier if you remember this easy guideline: Background fabric goes on the Board.

2. Press the piece as sewn to set the seam. This embeds the seam thread into the fabric. Not only does this reduce the bulk of the thread, it also warms the fabric for the next step.

3. Nudge the fabric open and gently finger-press the seam allowances toward the desired fabric. (It's easiest when you're pressing the top fabric away from yourself.) I think of this step as introducing the fabric to its new position.

Open the fabric and finger-press the seam.

4. Using the nose of the iron, gently push the top fabric into position, not really pressing down. The iron should be hovering slightly, applying just enough pressure to nudge the fabric into place.

5. Apply pressure straight down and then lift the iron. Continue nudging and pressing along the length of the strip. It's not fast; just take your time and enjoy the process.

Press along the seamline.

Pressing for a modern look

Pressing seams open is a new trend, embraced by the modern quilt movement. These relatively flat seams give a sleek, modern look to quilts, and they are especially appropriate for allover quilting designs. Although I find them much more challenging to line up for tight intersections, they are great for the more random piecing and overall quilting that's popular with the modern quilt crowd.

Pleats and grins

It is best to press fabric from the front rather than from the seam allowance side, where it's super easy to make a hash of things. Pleats in seams are some of our worst pressing gremlins. Even tiny pleats can add up—a sixteenth of an inch here, an eighth there. The next thing you know, nothing fits together, and it's usually our sewing that gets blamed for the problem.

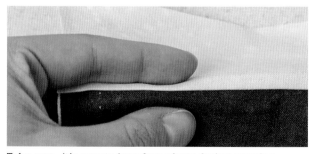

Take care—it's easy to introduce pleats during pressing.

Grinning seams are another problem. Usually the result of aggressive pressing, it's called "grinning" because the piecing threads show in the seams like a row of teeth. Keep a firm but gentle hand on that iron. A grinning seam also can be caused by the tension being set too loosely or by stitches that are too long. Ideally we should be able to piece with any color of thread without having it show in the seams.

Press gently to avoid "grinning" seams.

clipping seams

sneaky piecing tricks

After you've pressed the strips, cut them into segments, nested the seam allowances, and sewn the segments together, it's time to press the cross seam—but there's a problem. If you just press the seam to one side, half of the seam allowance will be pressed toward the background. That's no big deal if you're going to finish the quilt with an overall quilting design. But it *does* matter if you want to stitch in-the-ditch around these squares to accent a lovely pathway through the quilt.

If you clip the seam, you can flip each half away from the background. Working from the wrong side, make a little clip in the seam allowance just outside the seam intersection; it doesn't matter which side. Because this seam is on the straight of grain, make a diagonal clip; the bias won't fray. (On bias edges, clip straight in.) End the clip a few threads before the seamline—you don't want to cut through your seam.

Make a clip just outside the intersection of seams.

Now, working from the front, press the seam allowance away from the background. There will be a short length facing the wrong way, but that's okay. Nobody hits the ditch exactly right all the time anyway.

Clipping for Construction

Along with the rule of pressing away from the background, keep order of construction in mind. Plan to press the seams so they'll oppose each other for the cross seam.

Sometimes, no matter how carefully you plan, some seam allowances end up stacking instead of opposing. To get the tightest possible intersections, turn seams so they snuggle together; then clip the seam allowances to press them for the best appearance on the front of the quilt. I do this all the time!

Clip stacked seam allowances to press for a neat appearance.

flip-flop pressing

Take a look at the Homecoming block from *Do Re Mi* (page 65). After piecing all the subunits, it's time to make the block. Assembly-line sew the whole lot so they are strung together, and then take them to your pressing surface. It would be really lovely, wouldn't it, if the seam allowances in the middle of these blocks would oppose?

1. Decide which way you'd like the seams to be pressed. I'm all for pressing the seams toward the triangles.

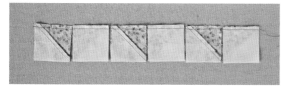

Place the strung-together pieces on the pressing board.

2. Stretch the string of pieces out on the pressing surface, with the seam side away from you. Remember the B Rule — "Background on the Board" (page 38)? Half of these units are in the right position; the other half, not so much. Flip those over to the correct position.

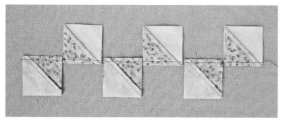

Flip every other piece to the right direction for pressing.

3. Now the units are set for simple pressing— one up, one down, one up, and so on. Set the seam, press, apply a little squirt of sizing, and press again.

4. Clip the threads *between* the blocks. You now have perfectly opposed seams with a thread pin to hold them together for the cross seam. How cool is that?

Pressing Triangles

To make sure half-square triangle units end up square, it's important to pay careful attention when pressing them.

1. Place the string of assembly-line-sewn half-square triangles on the pressing surface with the background fabric against the board.

2. Set the seams with your iron and then gently finger-press them to one side. Nudge the seams into place with your iron.

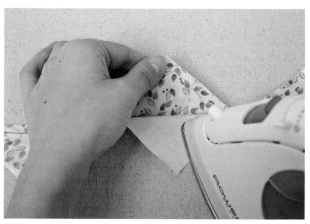

Nudge seams with the iron.

3. Dragging the iron along the seamline will pull the blocks out of square. Give them a little tug on the free corners to snap them back into square. With a little shot of sizing, they will be flat, crisp, and square.

"Snap" the blocks back to square.

Pressing Unsewn Biases

When pressing units with exposed bias edges, be very careful to keep the iron away from those edges so you don't stretch them out of shape. Press from the right-angle corner of the unit, and don't pull on any of the points.

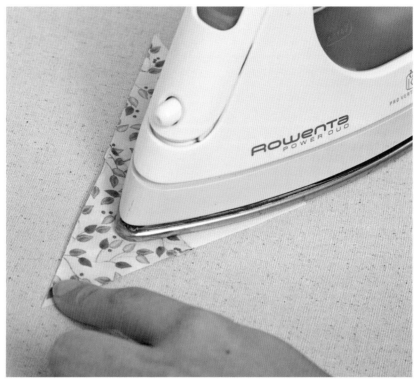

Press from the corner, avoiding the bias edge.

easy blocking

sneaky piecing tricks

Sometimes we have a block that just begs to be pressed out of shape. The skinny points on the *Mardi Gras* banner (page 89) are a perfect example. To keep these units square and true, I like to block the block.

1. Using a Sharpie ultrafine marker, draw a square on the ironing board cover to match the raw size of the unit.

2. Use heatproof glass-head pins to fasten the block within the square, pinning first at the corners and then at the center of each side. An application of spray sizing will relax the block and allow you to finger-press it into shape. Carefully press with a hot iron, using a straight down-and-up motion. Let the block cool a bit before you remove the pins.

Pin the block within the square drawn on the ironing surface.

sneaky new ways
to piece old favorites

Many favorite blocks appear time and again in our quilts. We love some for their simple assembly, others for their classic design—in spite of their difficulty. We're always on the prowl for easier ways to create the parts that create our quilts.

Sometimes "easier" isn't really easy—it's just a gimmick to sell us some gewgaw. My idea of a great trick is a way to piece a block without wasting time or fabric. It's also important to have the recipe to be able to use that method for any size block. This chapter is full of my favorite sneaky tricks—and foolproof recipes—for making quick work of old favorites.

Quilt design programs (I'm a big fan of Electric Quilt) are fun and addictive, but they don't include directions for sewing up the designs we create. The tricks and tips that follow will help you turn those designs into real quilts.

Shortcut Recipes for Blocks

We love shortcuts! We love sexy little gimmicks that get us to the finish line faster or more easily. These are my favorites sneaky tricks for making short work of troublesome blocks.

square in a square

sneaky piecing tricks

I love the Square in a Square block. It pairs up with other blocks so nicely, giving some terrific effects—as in *Sur la Table* (page 83). When it comes to sewing this block—well, that's another story. It's those dastardly triangles. To make room for the next seam allowance, they have to be big enough to make dog-ears on each side of the center square, which makes it a challenge to center them neatly. Let's make this block easy to sew.

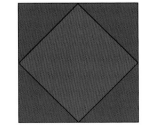

Square in a Square block

1. This block is made of 2 squares cut on the diagonal to make triangles, plus a larger square for the center. Carefully stack the triangles, right sides up, with the long side on the bottom.

Continued on next page

Continued from page 42

square in a square

sneaky piecing tricks

2. Fold the center square in half to make a rectangle, giving it a good crease. Lay it on the stack of triangles so that the fold touches the point at the top and the short side is even with the bottom.

3. Carefully flop the square open; it will be centered on the triangles. See those darned dog ears sticking out on either side of the square? Chop 'em off! You now have 4 triangles, perfectly trimmed to fit the center square, making this block a snap to sew. Cool beans!

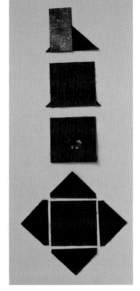

Center the folded square over the triangles, unfold, and then cut off the dog-ears.

THINKING ONCE: A TRIM TEMPLATE

All that stacking and folding isn't much of a shortcut if you're making dozens of blocks. A trim template lets you cut and trim your triangles in one quick pass. Cut the template to the raw dimensions of the center square and mark the centerline. Set it down on your cut triangles and nip those dog-ears away. Presto, you have perfectly trimmed triangles.

Match the centerline with the triangle points.

To make my template ultra-useful, I mark it with the finished block dimensions and the sizes to cut the center square and triangles.

Sewing the Square in a Square Block

Start by sewing triangles to opposite sides of the center square. Press the seams toward the triangles, and you're all good for lining up the next triangle. If you press them toward the center square, you'll lose your corner references for the next triangles. In that case, to get the third and fourth triangles in place, temporarily fold out the seam allowance, match up the trimmed triangle to the corner, and flop the seam allowance back toward the center square before sewing.

Match the triangle to the corner of the square.

The Recipe

The math for this block was challenging to figure out, but taken step by step, the formula—or recipe—is easy to follow.

Center square:

([Desired finished block size ÷ 2] × 1.414) + 0.5

Cut 1 square this size for the center of the Square in a Square block. The numbers will be kind of funky, so round to the nearest ⅛″.

Corner triangles:

(Desired finished block size ÷ 2) + 0.875

Cut 2 squares this size for each block; then cut in half diagonally and trim off the dog-ears.

five-square geese

Follow these steps to make five fabric squares into four Flying Geese. You'll use this technique for *Do Re Mi* (page 65), *Night Skies* (page 71), and *Sur la Table* (page 83).

Flying goose unit

Sewing the Block

Each goose is made up of 2 small triangles and a large triangle. The small triangles are half-squares; the larger one is a quarter-square. By changing the position of the background fabric, we can have either Flying Geese blocks (with the background fabric as the small triangles) or star points (with the background as the large triangle).

1. Position 2 small squares on opposite corners of the large square, right sides together, so that the lines drawn on the wrong sides connect. Yep, it's okay that the points overlap.

2. Stitch a seam ¼˝ on each side of the diagonal line. Cut on the line and press the seams away from the background fabric. You now have 2 funny-shaped hearts.

Place small squares in opposing corners, stitch, and cut apart.

3. Place one of the remaining small squares on each of the heart shapes, positioned so that the drawn line splits the cleavage of the heart.

4. Sew a seam ¼˝ from each side of the line. Cut along the line and press the seam allowances away from the background fabric. Voilà! You have 4 Flying Geese! How sneaky is that?

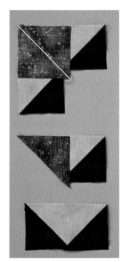

Stitch on the diagonal across the square, cut apart, and press.

The Recipe

For our formula to work, the finished geese need to be twice as long as they are tall.

Small triangles:
Desired finished size of the unit's short side + 0.875

Cut 4 squares this size. Mark a diagonal line from corner to corner on the wrong side of each square.

Large triangle:
Desired finished size of long side + 1.25

Cut 1 square.

fancy geese

sneaky piecing tricks

Let's have a little fun. We'll mix in some pieced units to see what we can stir up. Following the same steps as for constructing Flying Geese (page 44), for these Fancy Geese we'll substitute half-square triangle blocks for the small squares.

Fancy goose unit

Sewing the Block

Carefully position the half-square triangle patches on opposite corners of the large square and continue as you did for regular Flying Geese (Five-Square Geese, page 44). The fabric of the two half-square triangle patches that meets in the middle of the large square will become the triangles along the long side of the Fancy Geese block. The fabric placed at the corners of the large square will become the short sides of the Fancy Geese.

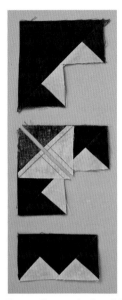

Fancy Geese piecing follows the same sequence as regular Flying Geese, but it uses half-square triangle patches for small squares.

The Recipe

Small triangles:

Desired finished size of short side + 1.25

1. Cut 2 squares this size from each color. Mark a diagonal line from corner to corner on the wrong side of each square.

2. Stack the squares in pairs, one of each color, right sides together. Stitch a seam ¼″ from the line on both sides. Cut on the line. Press the seams away from the background fabric. You now should have 4 half-square triangle patches the finished size of the short side plus 0.875.

3. Mark a diagonal line across the seam on the wrong side of each unit.

Large triangle:

Use the same formula as for the large triangle in the regular Flying Geese (Five-Square Geese, page 44).

tulip geese

You'll find this unit in *Mardi Gras* (page 89). Let's play with the big square this time. We're going to substitute a Square in a Square block for the plain large square in the regular Flying Geese block.

Tulip goose unit

Sewing the Block

Make a Square in a Square block following the instructions in Sneaky Trick: Square in a Square, (page 43).

Complete as you did for the basic Flying Geese (page 44), using the Square in a Square block as your large square.

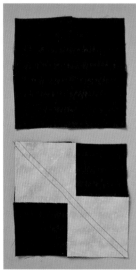

Give the goose a makeover by starting with a Square in a Square block.

Follow the steps for the regular Flying Geese.

The Recipe

Square in a Square center square:
([(Desired finished size of block long side + 0.75) ÷ 2] × 1.414) + 0.5

Round to the nearest ⅛˝.

In other words:

Start with the finished size for the long side of the goose.

Add 0.75 to get the finished size for your Square in a Square block.

Divide this number by 2.

Multiply the result by 1.414.

Add 0.5 to find the raw size of the center square. This is usually a pretty unwieldy number, so I round to the nearest ⅛˝. If in doubt, rounding up is better than rounding down.

Square in a Square corner triangles:
[(Finished size of long side + 0.75) ÷ 2] + 0.875

Cut 2 squares, and then cut each one in half on the diagonal.

Or:

Add 0.75 to the finished size of the long side of the goose.

Divide this number by 2.

Add 0.875.

Cut 2 squares this size, and then cut each in half on the diagonal to make half-square triangles.

Small triangles to complete the Tulip Geese:
Finished size of short side + 0.875

Cut 4 squares this size. Mark a diagonal line from corner to corner on the wrong side of each square.

sally's block

As with the Square in a Square block, a simple appearance doesn't necessarily mean simple to sew. I have a hard time with the triangles in this block. No matter how careful I am when pressing, the bias edges always seem to get warped out of shape. So here's a nice little workaround to avoid sewing cut biases. This block is found in *Sur la Table* (page 83).

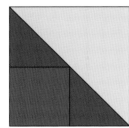

Sally's block

Sewing the Block

1. Sew strips for the corner square and small triangles together lengthwise. Press the seam away from the background.

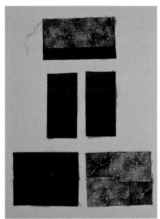

Join strip-set segments into lopsided four-patches.

2. Cut the strip set into segments the same width as the cut width of the corner-square strip; then sew the segments together to make stretched-out or lopsided four-patches. Yes, there's *supposed* to be a gap between corner squares. Make sure the corner squares are in the lower left and upper right corners of the four-patch; it really will make a difference.

3. Clip the seam right in the middle so that it can be pressed toward each corner square.

4. Place each large triangle rectangle on the table wrong side up, with a short side on the left. Align the 45° line on your ruler with the left edge of the rectangle so that it meets the upper left corner.

5. Use the edge of the ruler to draw a diagonal line from the upper left corner to the opposite side. The line will *not* extend into the opposite corner! Now rotate the rectangle and repeat at the opposite corner. Mark each rectangle the same way.

6. Layer the marked rectangles right sides together with the lopsided four-patches, making sure the lines are over the small triangle fabric in the four-patch, not over the corner square fabric. (See, it did matter!)

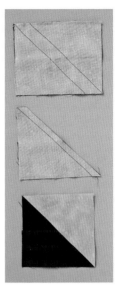

Mark the 45° diagonal, stitch, and trim.

7. Sew along both lines. Cut between the lines. Press the seams toward the large triangles. Ta-da!

The Recipe

Corner square:

[(Desired finished block size ÷ 2) + 0.5 = width to cut] × number of desired blocks = length of strip

Or:

Divide the desired finished block size by 2 and add 0.5. That's the width to cut. Multiply this by the number of desired blocks to get the strip length.

Small triangles:

(Desired finished block size ÷ 2) + 1.5 = width to cut. The required length is the same as for the corner squares.

Or:

Divide the desired finished block size by 2 and add 1.5. That's the width to cut. The length is the same as for the corner squares.

Large triangle:

(Desired finished block size + 0.5 tall) × (Desired finished block size + 1.5 wide)

Cut 1 rectangle this size for every 2 blocks you need.

Trim Templates for Skinny Points

When faced with blocks that have funny angles, we often turn to paper piecing. As I've said, paper piecing is not my friend. Beyond the issue of controlling the direction of the seam allowances, the whole flipping and visualizing process makes my head hurt, which left me in need of a strategy for piecing strange, pointy shapes.

The challenge comes from seam allowances that extend in unusual ways, making it a chore to get things aligned just so. We usually end up chopping the darned things off once the seam is sewn—so why not chop off the excess *before* we sew?

Look at the super-skinny points in our *Mardi Gras* banner (page 89). The trim templates are included in the pattern, but let me show you how they were designed. It's incredibly simple!

1. Start with a full-sized line drawing of the block. Cut it apart on the lines and paste the shapes onto another piece of paper at least ½˝ apart. Draw the ¼˝ seam allowance around each shape. Cut out the pieces.

2. On a lightbox, overlap the template shapes, right sides facing, as if you were going to sew them together. If you do not have a lightbox, you can tape the template shapes to a bright window. Be careful to align the original lines—that is, your seamline.

Draw the seam allowance around each piece.

3. See where the points on one template extend past the other template? Draw lines there and trim the excess away. Now you have your own trim template.

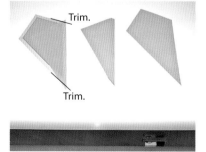

Trim.

Trim.

Paper or Plastic?

Making trim templates out of paper makes sense if you're making only a block or two, but template plastic is a good option if you are making a bunch. For trim templates that will be used for dozens of blocks, your local glass shop can cut an acrylic version. Just make sure to tell them that it has to match the template *exactly*. It will only cost a couple of bucks, and it will make the cutting process a whole lot easier.

Quilt Math

I love math. To be specific, I love algebra. As a kid, I relished story problems—sick, I know, but there you have it. After dabbling in all sorts of fiber techniques, it was the mathiness of quiltmaking that really sealed the deal for me. Figuring out yardages, cutting instructions, and order of construction are like the world's best story problem.

Quilt math doesn't have to be hard. To make just about any block in the quilt universe, there are only a few basic rules to remember.

- **Rule 1:** *Work with the finished size, adding the seam allowance at the end.*

  In other words, we need to break the block down into its most basic shapes, and only then do we add the seam allowances. Let's look at the Homecoming block from *Do Re Mi* (page 65). First, we

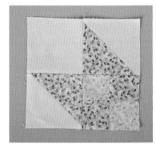

Figure out the finished size of each unit.

decide how big we want this block to finish. Just for grins, let's make it an 8˝ finished block.

We start by breaking it into parts. It's a four-patch made from three different units: a background square, 2 half-square triangles, and a smaller four-patch. To end up with an 8˝ × 8˝ block, each of these units needs to finish at 4˝ × 4˝. (Notice that we haven't carried along any seam allowances so far.)

- **Rule 2:** *To accommodate a ¼" seam allowance, the units need to have raw measurements ½" larger than the desired final measurements.*

We want the little four-patch to finish at 4" × 4". With two squares per side, we need to divide our finished size by 2, so that each of our little squares will finish at 2" × 2". We've broken this block down to its smallest components, so now we can add in the seam allowance. Each of the little squares will be cut at 2½". Good so far?

- **Rule 3:** *To cut half-square triangles from squares, add ⅞" to the desired finished size.*

To keep our points from getting chopped off in the cross seam, they need to finish ¼" out from the raw edge. The extra ⅞" will get us there.

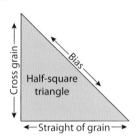

Going back to our *Do Re Mi* Homecoming block, we have 2 half-square triangle units that we want to finish at 4". Each unit is made up of a background fabric triangle and a triangle of another fabric. Each square we cut will net us 2 triangles. So we need one 4⅞" square of each fabric, which we'll cut in half on the diagonal to create our triangles.

- **Rule 4:** *For quarter-square triangles, add 1¼" to the desired finished measurement.*

With the stronger grain on the long side, quarter-square triangles are perfect to use as setting triangles for quilts set on point.

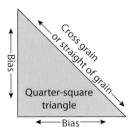

- **Rule 5:** *Count on about 40" of usable fabric from 42" to 44" quilting cottons.*

To determine how many shapes we can get from a strip cut the width of the fabric, we divide 40 by the raw size of the shapes.

The Rule of 14-14 for Setting Triangles

Sometimes we need to know how long the long side of our right triangles will be. This comes in handy when we want to figure out how big to cut the triangles that fill in the gaps on the edges of quilts set on point, or on the diagonal. It's important to cut these setting triangles so that the strongest grain is on the long edge, which makes them quarter-square triangles.

To determine their size, our magic number is 1.414. That's the square root of 2, and it's all about the formula $a^2 + b^2 = c^2$. Good old Pythagoras! Yep, we've tipped over into real math. But we can skip all that and just go straight to 1.414. I remember it as my rule of 14-14. Here it is:

Setting triangles:
(Desired finished block size × 1.414) + 1.25

Cut a square this size (round to the nearest ⅛"). Then cut in half diagonally twice (once in each direction) to make 4 triangles.

Mattress Sizes

Before we can decide how many blocks are needed for a quilt that's to go on a bed, we need to know how big the bed is. These are the standard measurements (width × length) for the top of a mattress:

Twin—39" × 75"
Extra-long twin—39" × 80"
Full—54" × 75"
Extra-long full—54" × 80"
Queen—60" × 80"
California queen—60" × 84"
King—76" × 80"
California king—72" × 84"

To cover the sides of the mattress—the "drop"—we need to add inches. On today's deep mattresses, the drop can be up to 17", which adds as much as 34" to the quilt dimensions. We need to add even more to cover a box spring, or if we want the quilt to go all the way to the floor.

the big finish

Whether we quilt by hand, machine, or checkbook (longarm quilters for hire are happy to let you help pay for their machines), taking the time to prepare the top will result in a prettier quilt. Once the piecing is done, it's time to add the borders and get the binding ready. This is our last chance to get the wrong side of our work put in order.

To Border or Not to Border?

The very worst reason to put a border on a quilt is to make it bigger. Back when I was working at the local quilt shop, quilters sometimes would arrive with something lap size and ask for help in making it queen size! My smart-aleck suggestion was that they make three more.

That said, wide borders—known as "slab-o-borders"—can be a wonderful way to showcase killer quilting designs. And there's no better way to show off extravagantly large-print fabrics.

measuring your borders

sneaky piecing tricks

Finding the correct measurement for border strips can be a hassle—and the bigger the quilt, the bigger the hassle. I don't know anyone who has a 90″ ruler, let alone a cutting mat that large. Most of us fall back on a tape measure, thumbing it along the quilt edges.

But as I've mentioned, seam allowances have a way of starting large and ending small. Those bigs and littles show up along the outer quilt edges, so measuring along the perimeter is hardly an accurate way to determine the correct length of a border. Instead, we want to measure through the center, cut the borders to that length, and ease in any discrepancy. But now we're back to not having an accurate way to measure.

Here's the thing. We don't need to know what the measurement is; we just need the border strips to match that measurement. So I let my piecing do the work.

1. Find a place to lay out your quilt top. I push the furniture aside and use my living room floor; in nice weather, the front yard works. My local quilt shop opens its classroom to customers between classes, or a church basement or library community room might be an option.

Continued on next page

Continued from page 50

sneaky piecing tricks

2. Start with the side. Stack up 2 border strips and square up an end. Pin the squared-up edges to the center top edge of the quilt. Smooth the strips over the quilt, and cut them even with the bottom quilt edge. Presto, you have perfectly sized border strips.

Measure top to bottom through the center of the quilt.

3. Fold the strips in half lengthwise and mark the fold with a pin; then fold in half again and mark the quarters. Pin the side border to the sides of the quilt, right sides together, matching the quilt center and quarters. Sew in place, easing as necessary.

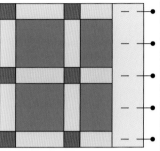

Pin on the side border, matching centers and quarters.

4. Press the seams. Traditionally they are pressed toward the border. However, if my borders are made of my background fabric, I may choose to press them toward the quilt.

5. Repeat with the top and bottom border strips, measuring side to side across the quilt center, including the side borders.

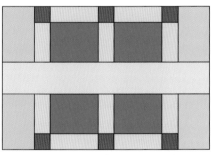

Measure side to side for the top and bottom border strips.

THINKING ONCE: SAFE PRESSING

I've found that when I set the nose of the iron to work correcting troublemaker seams, the heel of the iron is often busy messing up a whole bunch more. Use a Teflon or silicone pressing sheet to protect the happy seams while the naughty ones are being corrected.

A pressing sheet safeguards areas not being worked on.

Tidying Up the Quilt Top

Clipping Seams

Sometimes we clip seams to keep the background fabric in the background, sometimes because we've turned a seam to achieve a tight intersection. And sometimes we clip them because they turn when we're not looking. Lumpy seam allowances can throw off our free-motion quilting.

Now is also a great time to clip away any dog-ears that may have been missed in the piecing process.

Cleaning Up Loose Threads

The threads we use for construction are much fatter than the threads in the fabric. Trapped between the quilt top and the batting, these construction threads can actually wear away the fabric and eventually cut into the quilt top.

Dark threads trailing under fabric can shadow through as unsightly "varicose" threads. Trim them away before they can mar the quilt's beauty. If a thread or two get past you, use a super-fine crochet hook to carefully tease them out.

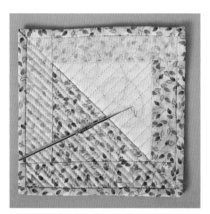

Use a crochet hook to pull out trapped threads.

After you've cleaned up the back, press the quilt top thoroughly. Working from the front, press carefully, using lots of spray sizing to make the fabric crisp and flat. If the quilt top is going to grow—I've seen it happen—you want the piecing pressed to its fullest size before you measure for the borders.

Making the Quilt Sandwich

Choosing the Backing

Once again, it's all about grainline for me. Whether a quilt is hung on the wall or pulled up under our chins on a chilly night, the biggest strain on the piecing is usually from top to bottom. Arranging the backing fabric so the straight of grain runs top to bottom helps protect the stitching.

Some suggest that a single seam up the middle of the quilt back is *très gauche*. They'd have us split one of our fabric lengths and sew half to each side of a center panel. In my universe, that just gives me one more seamline to cause trouble. I'm fine with a seam down the middle.

Truthfully, for large quilts, I'd just as soon spend the money on extra-wide backing fabric. If I *do* piece the backing, I make sure to remove the selvages and press the seams open.

Just to be safe, it's wise to cut the batting and backing larger than the quilt top. The larger the quilt, the more extra fabric I allow. For a queen-sized quilt, for example, I like an extra 3–4 inches on all sides. That means cutting the backing and batting an extra 6–8 inches wider and longer than the top. For smaller quilts, I usually just add an inch or 2 to each side.

Basting the Layers

Basting a quilt is my least favorite part of the process, but to be able to happily scribble my favorite free-motion patterns, the basting needs to be done well.

Begin by stabilizing the backing. For small wallhanging quilts, use masking tape to attach the backing (wrong side up) to the cutting mat. For bed quilts, a couple of banquet tables shoved together work well. (A library or church may be happy to share its tables.) Binder clips work better than tape for large backings. The fabric should be taut but not stretched.

The batting and quilt top aren't attached; rather, they "float" on the backing. Smooth them over the backing—first the batting and then the prepared quilt top. We have several choices for holding the layers together. Spray adhesives designed for quilt basting are available, but the cost is prohibitive for large quilts, and I don't like adding another chemical. Hand basting is common for hand quilting. For years, my quilts were pin basted—it wasn't unusual for me to use more than a thousand 1″ nickel-plated safety pins. Currently my favorite tool is a basting gun—the MicroStitch by Avery Dennison. The tacks are teeny tiny and soft enough to stitch through. With this tool, I can tack-baste a large quilt in less than an hour!

Quilting the Quilt

On most patterns, this is where we see those dreaded words, "Quilt as desired." Although it may seem cruel to leave it at that, there are simply too many options to fit into a pattern. Some will choose to hand quilt, others to quilt by machine. Some will want intricate patterns, while others will want to keep it simple.

The white background of *Do Re Mi* (page 65) was a perfect canvas for quilting fancy feather designs.

There's no shame in sending your quilt off to have someone else do the quilting. Think of it as your civic duty to the quilting community.

Blocking the Quilt

It was devastating—devastating, I tell you—the day I learned that the prize-winning quilters I so admired actually blocked their quilts for competition. Blocked, as in pinned to the floor and steamed into flat, square submission! I had always thought that these spectacular quilts were so well crafted that flat and square was in their DNA. All this time I'd been grieving over my own quilts, which were mostly flat and somewhat square.

Because I don't make quilts for competition, my idea of blocking involves a sunny day and a clothesline. Once a quilt is spread out on the bed, ready to cuddle away the chill, who gives a flip if it's perfectly square?

Wallhangings and competition quilts are a different story, though. To show them off at their best, we prefer that they not be too "friendly"—waving at everyone. We have a couple of ways to accomplish our goal.

Careful Piecing = Flatter Quilts

The first step, of course, is to take care while making the quilt. (Well, duh.) Paying attention to details all the way through construction, pressing carefully, correcting problems instead of stretching the fabric to fit, and minding our biases can go a long way toward creating a quilt that hangs beautifully. The quilting also needs to be uniform, without splotches of tightly packed designs amid loosely quilted areas.

If the design includes a wide border, consider adding an inch or two of width to give room for trimming to size. You'll again need an area big enough to lay out the quilt. Use a large ruler (I love my 20″ square for this) or carpenter's square to help get the corners just right. Slide a large cutting mat under the quilt edges, shifting it as necessary to trim away the excess. Some competition quilters even use a laser level.

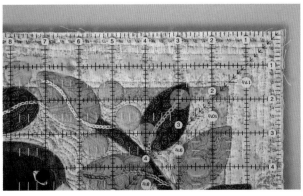

Trim as needed to square the corners.

Blocking with Steam

For a quilt that won't lie flat or that has no extra fabric for trimming, you'll need a space big enough to spread out the quilt. It's even better if the space is carpeted, which makes it pinnable.

Mark the center of each side with a sturdy pin; if it's a large quilt, also mark the quarters and even the eighths. Use the seamlines as reference, or fold the quilt to find the correct pin placement. Now would be a great time to use those yellow-headed "quilter's pins" you bought when you started quilting.

Pin the quilt to the carpet (I work with the backing side up), first the center top and then the center bottom, placing the pins exactly opposite each other. Now pin the center sides, making sure the line between the pins is perpendicular to the line between the top and bottom pins. Keep the quilt taut but not stretched.

Next place pins to the right of center top and bottom, then to the left of center top and bottom. Repeat along the sides, always placing new pins on both sides of pins already placed.

Carefully pin the quilt top in place for blocking.

Once the quilt is held in position, block it with steam. Use a garment steamer or an iron; the goal is to saturate the quilt with steam. When the quilt is fairly damp, use a dry iron to gently press the moisture away. Having the quilt face down protects the pretty side during this process. Carpeting will maintain the quilt's dimensionality. Allow the quilt to cool fully before removing the pins.

Some quilters like to wet their quilts fully, block them, and just let them air dry. But unless all the fabrics have tested colorfast (and sometimes in spite of it), colors tend to wick (migrate to their neighbors) when a quilt is left to air dry. The few times I've seen this happen, it was with fabrics that had been prewashed.

Bind and Admire

Quilt show judges get a bad rap for concentrating on binding. Having judged several major shows, I can tell you that's not where we start. But sometimes two quilts are so equally marvelous that we have to look for a way to distinguish one for the prize. How unfortunate that it often comes down to how the quilt is bound!

The binding is the last statement we get to make for a quilt. My favorite look is striped fabric cut on the bias. That barber-pole twist just seems happy and fun. A plaid cut on the bias gives a similar effect in a more country style.

Stripes and plaids make jaunty binding statements.

Bias grain is needed for binding quilts that have curvy edges. Otherwise, I avoid it like the plague. It's too stretchy and a major bother for binding plain old squares and rectangles. I prefer to cut my binding strips on the cross grain, which has enough give to keep the edges tight but isn't nearly as wobbly as bias-cut strips.

THINKING ONCE: BINDING DECISIONS

Have you ever found a hunk of fabric that you thought you'd been saving for a special purpose, but then decide you were mistaken and cut it to bits? Of course, that's when you remember that it was for binding one of your unfinished projects. Oh, the pain, the pain! So, even though making the binding is my least favorite part of a project, I make it first, roll it onto a toilet paper tube, and keep it with the quilt top.

Wind your binding onto a cardboard tube for safekeeping.

Regardless of the quilt's size, I usually cut my binding strips 2″ wide, which results in a narrow, tight binding that looks a little like piping.

Joining strips end to end with a diagonal seam reduces the bulk in the seam, giving a nicer finish to the quilt edges. Simply overlap the strip ends at a 90° angle, right sides together, and stitch on the diagonal. Trim the seam allowance to ¼″ and press open.

Trim the leading edge at a 45° angle and press a ¼″ seam allowance along the trimmed edge. Repeat with the opposite end of the binding, and you won't have to bother with finding the right end. Press the entire length in half lengthwise, wrong sides together.

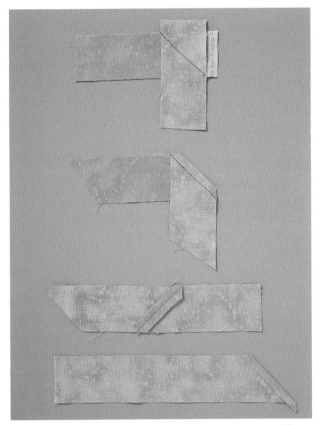

Seam strips diagonally, angle the end, and press under ¼″.

Applying the Binding

For the best finish, I prefer to apply the binding to the front of the quilt and hand-stitch the fold to the backing fabric. Before applying the binding, add a sleeve (page 58) or corner triangles (page 58) for hanging if desired.

1. Starting several inches from a corner, pin the pressed and angled seam allowance of the binding to the front of the quilt, right sides together and raw edges even. To leave room to tuck in the other end, begin your stitching a couple of inches from the start of the strip.

Begin stitching a couple of inches from the strip end.

2. This is a great time to use a walking (even-feed) foot to control all the layers. Having clear markings ¼″ in front of the needle also helps. Stitch ¼″ from the raw edges, stopping ¼″ from the corner. Turn the quilt 90° counterclockwise and stitch backward off the quilt edge.

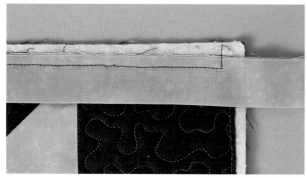

Turn and stitch off the quilt's edge.

3. Bring the binding around to match the raw edges on the new side. Tweak the fold so that it falls even with the previous raw edge.

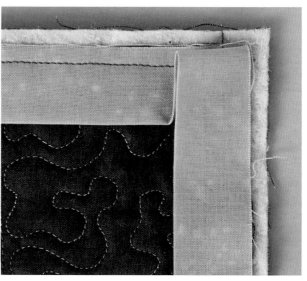

Fold to turn the binding to the next side.

4. Maintaining the same seam allowance, stitch from the quilt edge over the fold and down the side. Continue in the same fashion around the quilt top.

Stitch down the length of the new side.

5. For everyday quilts, I simply hack off the end of the binding, leaving just enough to stuff into the beginning end. For quilts that warrant a little more care, I trim the end at a 45° angle and tuck it into the opening. I slipstitch the ends closed.

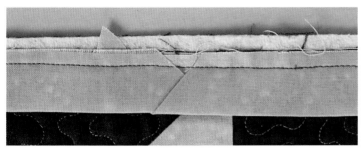

Slip the end of the strip into the opening.

6. Slipstitch the binding to the backing fabric to cover the seamline, using thread that matches the binding. I begin at the fold where the end has been inserted and take a couple of stitches to hold the ends in place.

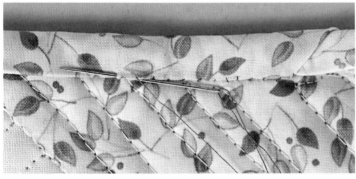

Slipstitch the binding along the fold.

7. For perfect corner miters on the back, make a couple of tacking stitches where the machine stitching crosses. Fold the binding to make a pretty miter and then catch the fold with a couple more tacking stitches. For a competition quilt, slipstitch the miter closed, front and back. At the beginning, a couple more stitches will close the join.

hiding the join

sneaky piecing tricks

When attaching the binding, start on the top edge of the quilt, especially if you're making the quilt for competition. The hanging sleeve will go along that edge. Most shows are judged after the quilts are hung, and few judges are tall enough to see the top edge. I'm just saying.

Washing Your Quilt

For my "baby's" first bath, I take extra care. After that, the bed quilts are tossed in the washer and hung on the line to dry. Nothing smells better than a quilt that's been dried outside.

For the first wash, I set the washing machine on normal cycle with the water temperature on cold/cold, and I don't use soap. (Marking pens and pencils can be set by heat and soap.) Then I give the quilt a good once-over to make sure all the marking lines are gone and no colors have run. If everything's okay, I toss it back into the washer—again on normal cycle, but this time on warm/cold and using detergent.

I'm a big fan of Orvus Paste (aka Orvus WA Paste). Essentially a horse shampoo, it's sold by the gallon at a farm supply store near where I live. Quilt shops stock it in smaller containers, prosaically called Quilt Soap. Orvus lacks the brightening and whitening additives that can be so wearing on fabrics. Just a dab—a tablespoon max—is all that's needed to produce a sparklingly clean quilt. I'm a maverick and use Downy fabric softener in the rinse. This is probably not the best idea for competition quilts, because softeners can attract dirt, but it sure makes my bed quilts nice for cuddling.

I remove the quilt from the washer and inspect it. If all is well, I pop it into the dryer for a nice hot tumble until it's bone dry. Because I don't prewash my cotton fabrics and batting, the quilt will come out looking rather shriveled and puckered. So into the washer it goes one more time—this time with fabric softener for sure (detergent is optional). At last the quilt is ready for my kind of blocking: a lazy afternoon, drying on the line in dappled sunshine.

easy hanging solutions

I tend to think of big quilts as being for beds, but some people like to hang them so that even those without an invitation to the bedroom can admire them.

Café rings. My favorite way to hang quilts doesn't require any extra sewing at all. Instead, I use a decorative curtain rod and café rings. Quilts can be changed easily from season to season, and if they have an allover design, it's easy to rotate them, reducing stress on the fabric.

Corner triangles. For smaller quilts, my favorite hanging method is corner triangles, a technique I learned from quilting author and teacher Ami Simms:

1. Out of scraps from the project, cut 2 squares 4″ × 4″. (The fabric scraps don't have to match.) Press each in half on the diagonal, wrong sides together, to make 2 triangles.

2. Pin the square corners of the triangles to the backing side of the quilt top, raw edges even. Machine-baste in place, and then apply the quilt binding.

3. Cut a yardstick to fit between the triangles. If the quilt is wider than a yardstick, you can use a furring strip, which is available at a hardware store or home center. A dowel also works.

4. Attach a sawtooth picture hanger to the center of the yardstick. Slip the ends of the yardstick under the triangles and hang the quilt. (If you're using a dowel, just perch it on 2 nails in the wall.)

Slide the yardstick into the corner triangles.

Ready-made sleeves. Ask at your local quilt shop for this terrific new product called Quilters Hangup. For a few dollars, you can buy a yard of ready-made sleeve. Just pin and sew it in place.

Making a Hanging Sleeve

If you want to make an honest-to-goodness hanging sleeve for your quilt, here's how:

1. Before you bind the quilt, cut a fabric rectangle 9″ tall and as wide as the quilt. Turn under the short ends ¼″. Turn under again and stitch.

2. Fold the strip lengthwise, wrong sides together, offsetting the raw edges by about ½″. Press.

3. With the shorter side of the sleeve against the quilt, realign the sleeve's raw edges and center the strip along the quilt top. Machine-baste the top edge, using a very narrow seam that won't show in front.

4. Bind the quilt. Being careful that your stitches don't show in front, whipstitch the creased edge of the sleeve to the quilt back. (The side of the sleeve facing out will be a little loose, leaving room for the hanging rod.) Stitch down the sleeve's backing side ends to keep the rod from slipping behind them.

make mine argyle

FINISHED SIZE: 77½″ × 93″

Designed, pieced, and quilted by Beth Ferrier

Sharpen your cutting and sewing skills on this charmingly simple quilt. Plain blocks cut from a single fabric are alternated with pieced blocks and framed with pieced edging units. This makes the perfect quilt for a college dorm room's twin-size bed.

Fabrics used in this quilt

materials

Yardage is based on 40˝-wide fabric. Yardage amounts have been rounded up to include a little wiggle room.

3⅓ yards large-scale print for background

2½ yards of another background print for blocks

½ yard fabric in Light Accent Color 1

½ yard fabric in Dark Accent Color 1

½ yard fabric in Light Accent Color 2

½ yard fabric in Dark Accent Color 2

⅓ yard fabric in Accent Color 3

⅞ yard striped fabric for binding

Backing fabric and batting sized for quilt

6 quart-size zip-top plastic bags, labeled 1–6

1 gallon-size zip-top plastic bag, labeled 7

Rotary cutter, mat, and ruler (16½˝ square recommended)

cutting

WOF = width of fabric

As you cut, you'll organize your cut pieces into bags as indicated.

▢ *large-scale print*

Cut 6 strips 15½˝ × WOF. Subcut:

  13 rectangles 15½˝ × 13˝.
  4 rectangles 15½˝ × 8˝.

Cut 1 strip 13˝ × WOF. Subcut:

  4 rectangles 13˝ × 9½˝.

Cut 1 strip 8˝ × WOF. Subcut:

  4 rectangles 8˝ × 9½˝.

Place all of these pieces in Bag 7.

▢ *background print for blocks*

Cut 7 strips 3½˝ × WOF. Subcut:

  84 rectangles 3½˝ × 3˝. *Place 6 each in Bags 1 and 3, 12 each in Bags 2 and 4, and 24 each in Bags 5 and 6.*

Cut 3 strips 9½˝ × WOF. Subcut:

  30 rectangles 9½˝ × 3˝. *Place 2 in Bag 1, 4 in Bag 2, and 12 each in Bags 5 and 6.*

Cut the remainder of the last strip to 8˝ × about 28˝. Subcut:

  8 rectangles 8˝ × 3½˝. *Place 2 each in Bags 3 and 4, and place 4 in Bag 5.*

Cut 2 strips 8″ × WOF. Subcut:

> 22 rectangles 8″ × 3½″. *Place 2 in Bag 4, 8 in Bag 5, and 12 in Bag 6.*

Cut 1 strip 6½″ × WOF. Subcut:

> 12 rectangles 6½″ × 3″. *Place 4 in Bag 3 and 8 in Bag 4.*

Cut 2 strips 5½″ × WOF. Subcut:

> 12 rectangles 5½″ × 3½″. *Place 4 in Bag 1 and 8 in Bag 2.*

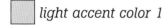 *light accent color 1*

Cut 4 strips 3½″ × WOF. Subcut:

> 40 rectangles 3½″ × 3″. *Place 8 each in Bags 2 and 4, and place 12 each in Bags 5 and 6.*

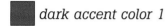 *dark accent color 1*

Cut 4 strips 3½″ × WOF. Subcut:

> 40 rectangles 3½″ × 3″. *Place 8 each in Bags 2 and 4, and place 12 each in Bags 5 and 6.*

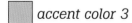 *light accent color 2*

Cut 3 strips 3½″ × WOF. Subcut:

> 32 rectangles 3½″ × 3″. *Place 4 each in Bags 1 and 3, and place 12 each in Bags 5 and 6.*

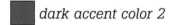 *dark accent color 2*

Cut 3 strips 3½″ × WOF. Subcut:

> 32 rectangles 3½″ × 3″. *Place 4 each in Bags 1 and 3, and place 12 each in Bags 5 and 6.*

 *accent color 3*

Cut 2 strips 3½″ × WOF. Subcut:

> 24 rectangles 3½″ × 3″. *Place 2 each in Bags 1 and 3, 4 each in Bags 2 and 4, and 6 each in Bags 5 and 6.*

striped fabric

A total of 350″ of 2″-wide bias for binding (Refer to Bind and Admire, page 54.) *Place in Bag 7.*

Instructions

Unless otherwise noted, all seam allowances are ¼″, and pieces are sewn right sides together. Seams are always pressed away from the background fabric (AFTB).

Whew! That was a lot of cutting, but now all your pieces are organized and waiting for you. No fumbling around, looking for the right parts!

This quilt is made up of simple shapes; the color placement makes the design sing. To create the stretched-out blocks, you'll be working with rectangles instead of traditional squares. The rectangles will be tall (vertical) in some blocks and short (horizontal) in others. Watch for that, and you'll be all good.

Making the Pieced Edging Units

To see how the following units will be placed on the quilt top, refer to the assembly diagram (page 64).

Unit A

Make 2 of these units for the side edging, using the pieces in Bag 1. They include Light Accent Color 2, Dark Accent Color 2, and Accent Color 3 fabrics.

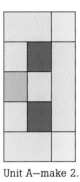

Unit A—make 2.

1. Use 12 rectangles 3″ × 3½″ (6 of the block background print, 4 of Dark Accent Color 2, and 2 of Accent Color 3). Assembly-line sew them into pairs for the inner six-patch section of the unit, as shown. Flip-flop press (page 40) the pieces. Cut the threads between, not within, the units.

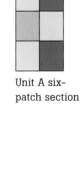

Unit A six-patch section

Join the pairs with assembly-line sewing.

2. Sew the stitched pairs together to make the six-patch section. Press the seams AFTB, clipping as needed.

3. Add 1 background print rectangle 9½″ × 3″, 2 background print rectangles 3″ × 5½″, and 2 Light Accent Color 2 rectangles 3″ × 3½″. The corners of the six-patch sections should match up exactly with the corners of the Light Accent Color 2 rectangles. If they don't, refer to Sneaky Trick: Check Sum (page 24) to sort it all out.

4. Press the seams. The 2 units should each measure 8″ × 15½″. Label them A.

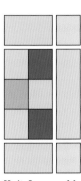

Unit A assembly diagram

Unit B

Wasn't that fun? Let's do it again using the Light and Dark Accent Colors 1 and the Accent Color 3 fabrics.

Make 4 of these units for the side edging, using the pieces in Bag 2 and repeating Steps 1–4 for Unit A (page 61). Each unit should measure 8″ × 15½″. Label these B.

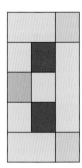

Unit B

Unit C

Make 2 of these units for the top and bottom edging, using the pieces in Bag 3 (background print, Light and Dark Accent Color 2, and Accent Color 3 fabrics).

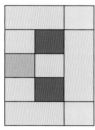

Unit C

These units are pieced exactly the same as Units A and B, *except* you'll be sewing horizontally oriented rectangles this time.

1. Using 3½″ × 3″ rectangles, sew together 2 six-patch sections as shown, following the directions in Steps 1 and 2 for Unit A. Press.

Unit C six-patch section

2. Add 2 background print rectangles 3″ × 6½″, 1 background print rectangle 3½″ × 8″, and 2 Light Accent Color 2 rectangles 3″ × 3½″ to each six-patch section, as in Step 3 for Unit A. The finished units should measure 9½″ × 13″. Label them C, and add them to your pile of lettered units.

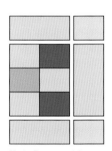

Unit C assembly diagram

Unit D

Now repeat the same process (Steps 1 and 2 for Unit C) to make 4 units for the top and bottom edging, using the pieces in Bag 4 (background print, Light and Dark Accent Color 1, and Accent Color 3 fabrics). The finished units should measure 9½″ × 13″. Label them D.

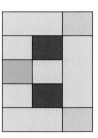

Unit D

Making the Blocks

Now you're ready to make the E and F pieced blocks. They are both sewn the same way; the only difference is the placement of the accent color fabrics within the blocks. When you lay out all the blocks, you'll see how they create a pattern.

Block E

Make 6 of these blocks for the top and bottom center of the quilt top, using the pieces in Bag 5. Use matching accent fabrics in the 2 upper corners and in the 2 bottom corners.

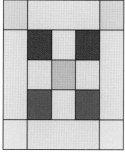

Block E

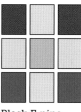

THINKING ONCE: LAY IT ALL OUT

Save yourself some heartache: Remember to think once and lay out all the pieces for the block before you begin sewing. Start by assembly-line sewing (page 23) the left vertical seams. Press the seams AFTB—you know what that means!

1. Sew together the inner bunch of rectangles just as you did for Unit A (page 61). This time follow the Block E assembly diagram to make a nine-patch instead of the usual six-patch.

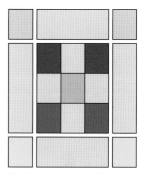

Block E nine-patch unit

2. Make 6 six-patch sections using the left-hand and center columns of the nine-patch units. Follow Steps 1 and 2 for Unit A.

3. To complete the nine-patch, add the column of rectangles to the right side of the unit from Step 2. Press the seams. The nine-patch units should now each measure 8″ × 9½″.

4. Assembly-line sew the cross seams.

5. Add the outer rectangles. The finished blocks should measure 13″ × 15½″. Label them E.

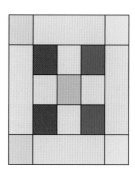

Block E assembly diagram

Block F

Same song, different verse. Make 6 blocks using the pieces in Bag 6, following the same sequence as for Block E, but this time using matching fabrics in the 2 left corners and in the 2 right corners.

These blocks should measure 13″ × 15½″. Label them F.

Block F

Assembling the Quilt Top

Gather all the lettered units and blocks you've pieced, plus all the pieces from Bag 7. The pieces from Bag 7 include both plain cut blocks and plain edging units. Now push back the furniture to make a nice place for laying out all the parts of your quilt top.

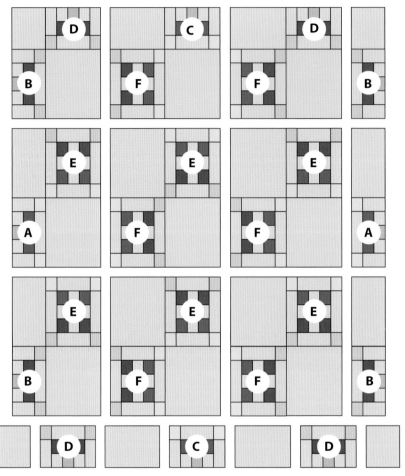

Quilt top assembly diagram

1. Refer to the assembly diagram to lay out the units, paying close attention to fabric placement. Blocks E and F will need to be turned this way and that to get the colors to line up properly.

2. Sew the blocks and edging units together as shown to make larger blocks; press.

3. Sew the large blocks into rows; press. Then sew together the rows. Give the top a final press.

Finishing the Quilt

Refer to The Big Finish (page 50) for guidelines on layering, quilting, blocking, and binding your quilt.

do re mi

FINISHED SIZE: 90″ × 90″

Designed, pieced, and quilted by Beth Ferrier

Jam-packed with sneaky piecing tricks, this project is a fantastic place for beginning quilters to graduate into confident beginners. Boldly graphic, this quilt would look great in any color combination.

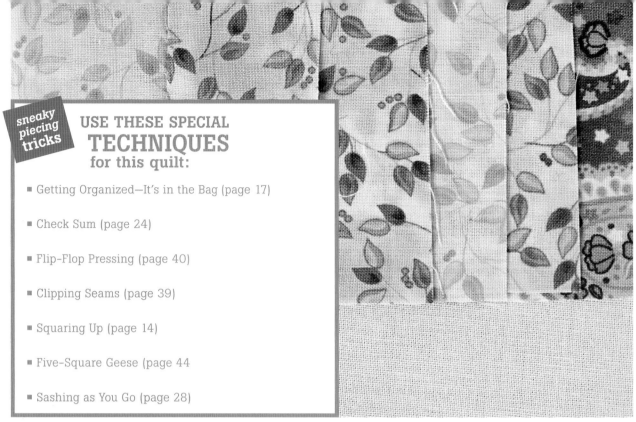

USE THESE SPECIAL TECHNIQUES
for this quilt:

- Getting Organized—It's in the Bag (page 17)

- Check Sum (page 24)

- Flip-Flop Pressing (page 40)

- Clipping Seams (page 39)

- Squaring Up (page 14)

- Five-Square Geese (page 44

- Sashing as You Go (page 28)

Fabrics used in this quilt

materials

Yardage is based on 40"-wide fabric unless otherwise noted. Yardage amounts have been rounded up to include a little wiggle room.

4⅞ yards* background fabric (A) for pieced blocks

1½ yards green fabric (B) for pieced blocks

⅞ yard yellow fabric (C) for pieced blocks

1 yard red fabric (D) for pieced blocks

1½ yards blue fabric (E) for pieced blocks and binding

Backing fabric and batting sized for quilt

10 gallon-size zip-top bags, labeled 1–10

Rotary cutter, mat, and ruler (20½" square recommended)

*Requires 42" usable fabric width.

cutting

WOF = width of fabric

As you cut, you'll organize your cut pieces into bags as indicated.

background fabric (A)

Cut 6 strips 5⅞" × WOF. Subcut:

　32 squares 5⅞" × 5⅞". Mark the diagonal on the wrong side. *Place in Bag 4.*
　2 squares 5½" × 5½". *Place in Bag 7.*

Cut 7 strips 5½" × WOF. Subcut:

　44 squares 5½" × 5½". *Place 16 in Bag 6, 4 in Bag 7, and 24 in Bag 9.*

Cut 1 strip 11¼" × WOF. Subcut:

　3 squares 11¼" × 11¼". *Place in Bag 5.*

Cut 1 strip 10½" × WOF. Subcut:

　4 squares 10½" × 10½". *Place in Bag 9.*

Cut 1 strip 25½" × WOF. Subcut:

　12 rectangles 25½" × 3". *Place in Bag 10.*

Cut 7 strips 6¾" × WOF. Subcut:

  4 segments 6¾" × 40½".

  2 segments 6¾" × 30½".

  2 segments 6¾" × 18".

  Place all in Bag 10.

green fabric (B)

Cut 6 strips 5⅞" × WOF. Subcut:

  32 squares 5⅞" × 5⅞". *Place in Bag 4.*

  4 squares 5½" × 5½". *Place in Bag 8.*

Cut 2 strips 5⅞" × WOF. Subcut:

  12 squares 5⅞" × 5⅞". Mark the diagonal on the wrong side. *Place in Bag 5.*

yellow fabric (C)

Cut 2 strips 5½" × WOF. Subcut:

  16 rectangles 5½" × 3". *Place in Bag 1.*

Cut 5 strips 3" × WOF. *Place 2 in Bag 3.*

  From the remaining 3 strips, subcut:

  36 squares 3" × 3". *Place in Bag 2.*

red fabric (D)

Cut 4 strips 5½" × WOF. Subcut:

  16 rectangles 5½" × 3". *Place in Bag 1.*

  16 squares 5½" × 5½". *Place in Bag 1.*

  4 squares 3" × 3". *Place in Bag 2.*

Cut 2 strips 3" × WOF. *Place in Bag 3.*

blue fabric (E)

Cut 8 strips 3" × WOF. *Place 4 in Bag 3.*

  From the remaining 4 strips, subcut:

  49 squares 3" × 3". *Place 40 in Bag 2 and 9 in Bag 10.*

Cut 10 strips 2" × WOF for the binding. *Place in Bag 10.*

Instructions

Unless otherwise noted, all seam allowances are ¼", and pieces are sewn right sides together. Seams are always pressed away from the background fabric (AFTB).

Pieced-Square Units

Make 16 of these units, using the pieces in Bag 1.

1. With right sides together, assembly-line sew (page 23) the long sides of the fabric D to the fabric C 5½" × 3" rectangles. Press the seam toward fabric D.

Join the long sides of the rectangles.

2. Match this pieced square to the 5½" square D. Are they the same size? If not, see Sneaky Trick: Check Sum (page 24).

3. Sew the rectangle C side of the pieced square from Step 1 to square D as shown. Press the seam toward fabric D. The pieces should measure 5½" × 10½". *Place in Bag 8.*

Sew the pieced square to square D. Make 16.

Four-Patches

1. Use the pieces in Bag 2, starting with 4 of the D squares, 4 of the C squares, and 8 of the E squares. Think once by laying out a template layer (page 22) of fabric pieces for the four-patch; stack the remaining squares on top.

Make 4 of these four-patches.

2. Use assembly-line sewing to join the squares. Flip-flop press (page 40) the seams away from fabric D.

3. Sew the cross seams, clipping as needed and pressing away from fabric D. *Place these 4 four-patches in Bag 7.*

4. Repeat Steps 1–3 to make 16 more four-patches with the remaining C and E squares in Bag 2, pressing the seams toward fabric C. *Place these units in Bag 6.*

Make 16 of these four-patches.

Border Six-Packs

Make 12 units using the pieces in Bag 3.

1. Make 2 strip sets with the 3″ strips of fabrics D and E as shown. Press the seams away from fabric E. Cut into 12 segments 5½″ each.

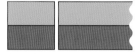

Cut 12 segments each 5½″ wide.

2. Make 2 strip sets with the 3″ strips of fabrics C and E. Press the seams away from fabric E. Cut into 24 segments 3″ wide.

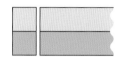

Cut 24 segments each 3″ wide.

3. Sew a 3″-wide C/E segment to each side of the 5½″-wide D/E segments. The six-pack units should now measure 5½″ × 10½″. *Place in Bag 9.*

Make 12 pieced six-pack units.

Half-Square Triangles

Make 64 of these units, using the pieces in Bag 4. Note that the background fabric squares are marked in half diagonally on the wrong side.

1. Layer 1 each of fabric A and B squares, right sides together. Sew ¼″ on both sides of the marked diagonal line.

2. Cut on the marked line; press the seams toward the fabric B triangles. *Place 32 in Bag 6, 8 in Bag 7, and 24 in Bag 9.*

Sew ¼″ from diagonal, cut, and press. Make 64.

Center Homecoming Block

Make 16 blocks, using the pieces in Bag 6. The blocks will be 10½″ square.

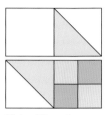

1. Lay out a template layer and stack the remaining units on top, 16 pieces in each stack.

2. Assembly-line sew the pieces and flip-flop press the seams away from fabric A (the background fabric), which will be next to the fabric B triangles.

Make 16 center blocks.

3. Sew the cross seams; press. *Place in Bag 8.*

- -

Border Homecoming Block

Repeat the center Homecoming block steps to make 4 border blocks, using the pieces in Bag 7. *Place in Bag 9.*

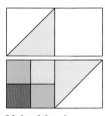

Make 4 border blocks.

- -

Flying Geese

Create 12 Flying Geese units from the 5⅞″ × 5⅞″ fabric B squares and the 11¼″ × 11¼″ fabric A squares, using the Five-Square Geese technique (page 44). *Place these in Bag 9.*

Make 12 Flying Geese.

Assembling the Do-Re-Mi Block

1. Take the pieces from Bag 8 and lay out a template layer of the Do-Re-Mi block. Stack the remaining units on top.

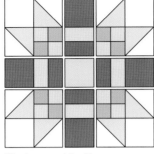

Block assembly diagram; make 4.

2. Assembly-line sew the first vertical seam. Flip-flop press toward the pieced rectangle units.

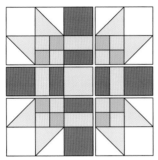

Start with the vertical seams on the left.

3. Assembly-line sew the remaining vertical seams. Flip-flop press.

4. Sew the cross seams. The blocks should measure 25½″ × 25½″. *Place in Bag 10.*

Sew the vertical seams on the right.

Assembling the Quilt Center

Using the pieces and units in Bag 10, assemble the quilt center.

1. Referring to the instructions for Sashing as You Go (page 28), add the 25½″ × 3″ fabric A sashing and the 3″ × 3″ cornerstones.

2. Join each 6¾″ × 18″ fabric A segment to a 6¾″ × 40½″ fabric A segment, end to end, to form the side borders of the quilt center. Press. Sew in place.

3. Join each 6¾″ × 30½″ fabric A segment to a 6¾″ × 40½″ fabric A segment to form the top and bottom borders for the quilt center. Sew in place.

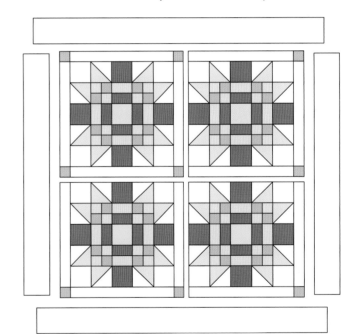

Quilt center assembly diagram

Borders and Binding

Use the Bag 9 pieces to make the borders.

1. Using the Flying Geese, the six-pack units, the half-square triangles, and the 5½″ × 5½″ fabric A squares, make 12 border half-blocks. Press the seams away from fabric A.

Make 12 half-blocks.

2. Join 2 of the half-blocks and a 10½″ × 10½″ background fabric square end to end as shown. Make 4—2 for the top and bottom borders and 2 for the centers of the side borders.

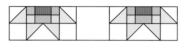

Sew the half-blocks to the background fabric squares. Make 4.

3. Use 2 units from Step 2 for the center of each side border, adding a Border Homecoming Block (page 68) at each end. To finish the top and bottom borders, add the remaining half-blocks from Step 1 at each end of each border. Make sure the units are turned properly.

Assemble the side borders.

4. Join the side borders and then the top and bottom borders to the quilt center. Press carefully.

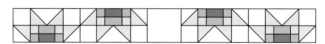

Assemble the top and bottom borders.

Finishing the Quilt

Refer to The Big Finish (page 50) for guidelines on layering, quilting, blocking, and binding your quilt.

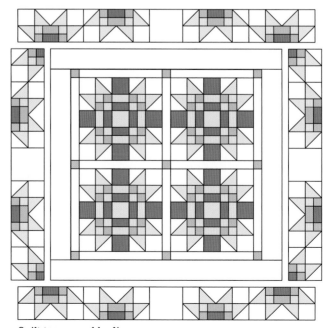

Quilt top assembly diagram

night skies

FINISHED SIZE: 64″ × 84″

Designed, pieced, and quilted by Beth Ferrier

Large, simple blocks—put together using some of the best sneaky piecing tricks around—make this quilt an easy weekend project. Make it for one of the superstars in your life.

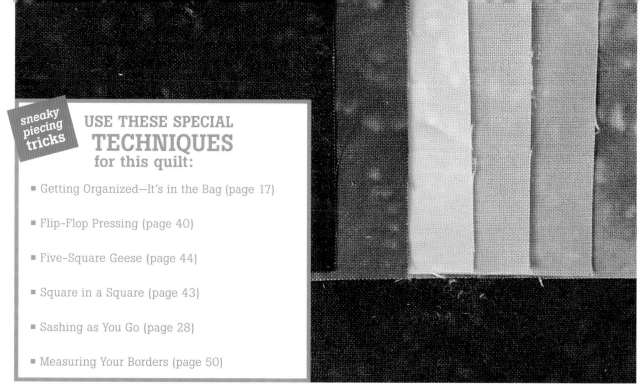

 (caption below the image)

Fabrics used in this quilt

sneaky piecing tricks

USE THESE SPECIAL
TECHNIQUES
for this quilt:

- Getting Organized—It's in the Bag (page 17)

- Flip-Flop Pressing (page 40)

- Five-Square Geese (page 44)

- Square in a Square (page 43)

- Sashing as You Go (page 28)

- Measuring Your Borders (page 50)

Fabrics used in this quilt

materials

Yardage is based on 40″-wide fabric unless otherwise noted. Yardage amounts have been rounded up to include a little wiggle room.

4 yards* background fabric for pieced blocks

1 yard dark red fabric for pieced blocks and binding

⅓ yard bright blue fabric for pieced blocks

⅓ yard lemon yellow fabric for pieced blocks

⅞ yard yellow fabric for pieced blocks

⅓ yard dark yellow fabric for pieced blocks

⅞ yard orange fabric for pieced blocks

Backing fabric and batting sized for quilt

7 gallon-size zip-top bags, labeled 1–7

Rotary cutter, mat, and ruler (a 12½″ square ruler is handy)

3⅜″ square of template plastic *(Place in Bag 3.)*

*Requires 41″ usable fabric width.

cutting

WOF = width of fabric

As you cut, you'll organize your cut pieces into bags as indicated.

background fabric

Cut 3 strips 9¼″ × WOF. Subcut:

 12 squares 9¼″ × 9¼″. *Place in Bag 1.*

Cut 13 strips 4½″ × WOF. Subcut:

 4 segments 4½″ × 40½″.* *Place in Bag 7.*

From each of 2 remaining strips, subcut:

 1 segment 4½″ × 36½″.* *Place in Bag 7.*
 1 square 4½″ × 4½″. *Place in Bag 5.*

From each of 2 remaining strips, subcut:

 1 segment 4½″ × 24½″.* *Place in Bag 7.*
 3 squares 4½″ × 4½″. *Place in Bag 5.*

From the 5 remaining strips, subcut:

 40 squares 4½″ × 4½″. *Place in Bag 5.*

*Finished quilt dimensions can vary. Refer to Sneaky Trick: Measuring Your Borders (page 50) before cutting these pieces.

Cut 5 strips 6½″ × WOF. Subcut:

  34 rectangles 6½″ × 4½″. *Place 24 in Bag 6 and 10 in Bag 7.*

Cut 6 strips 2⅞″ × WOF. Subcut:

  70 squares 2⅞″ × 2⅞″. *Place 46 in Bag 3 and 24 in Bag 2.*

dark red fabric

Cut 1 strip 4½″ × WOF. Subcut:

  6 squares 4½″ × 4½″. *Place in Bag 4.*

  4 squares 2⅞″ × 2⅞″. Mark the diagonal on the wrong side. *Place in Bag 2.*

Cut 1 strip 3⅜″ × WOF. Subcut:

  6 squares 3⅜″ × 3⅜″. *Place in Bag 3.*

Cut 2 strips 2⅞″ × WOF. Subcut:

  20 squares 2⅞″ × 2⅞″. Mark the diagonal on the wrong side. *Place in Bag 2.*

Cut 8 strips 2″ × WOF for the binding. *Place in Bag 7.*

lemon yellow fabric

Cut 1 strip 4½″ × WOF. Subcut:

  3 squares 4½″ × 4½″. *Place in Bag 7.*

  10 squares 2½″ × 2½″. Mark the diagonal on the wrong side. *Place in Bag 6.*

Cut 1 strip 2½″ × WOF. Subcut:

  14 squares 2½″ × 2½″. Mark the diagonal on the wrong side. *Place in Bag 6.*

bright blue fabric

Cut 2 strips 3⅜″ × WOF. Subcut:

  17 squares 3⅜″ × 3⅜″. *Place in Bag 3.*

yellow fabric

Cut 3 strips 4⅞″ × WOF. Subcut:

  24 squares 4⅞″ × 4⅞″. Mark the diagonal on the wrong side. *Place in Bag 1.*

Cut 1 strip 5¼″ × WOF. Subcut:

  6 squares 5¼″ × 5¼″. *Place in Bag 2.*

Cut 2 strips 2½″ × WOF. Subcut:

  24 squares 2½″ × 2½″. *Place in Bag 4.*

dark yellow fabric

Cut 1 strip 4½″ × WOF. Subcut:

  3 squares 4½″ × 4½″. *Place in Bag 7.*

  10 squares 2½″ × 2½″. Mark the diagonal on the wrong side. *Place in Bag 6.*

Cut 1 strip 2½″ × WOF. Subcut:

  14 squares 2½″ × 2½″. Mark the diagonal on the wrong side. *Place in Bag 6.*

orange fabric

Cut 3 strips 4⅞″ × WOF. Subcut:

  24 squares 4⅞″ × 4⅞″. Mark the diagonal on the wrong side. *Place in Bag 1.*

Cut 1 strip 5¼″ × WOF. Subcut:

  6 squares 5¼″ × 5¼″. *Place in Bag 2.*

Cut 2 strips 2½″ × WOF. Subcut:

  24 squares 2½″ × 2½″. *Place in Bag 4.*

Instructions

Unless otherwise noted, all seam allowances are ¼˝, and pieces are sewn right sides together. Seams are always pressed away from the background fabric (AFTB).

Big Geese Units

Using the Five-Square Geese method (page 44) and the pieces in Bag 1, make 24 orange/background and 24 yellow/background Flying Geese units. These should measure 4½˝ × 8½˝. *Place in Bag 5.*

Make 24 of each.

Small Geese Units

1. Using the Five-Square Geese method and the pieces in Bag 2, make 24 background/orange Flying Geese. These units should measure 2½˝ × 4½˝.

2. Repeat Step 1 to make 24 dark red/yellow Flying Geese. Press the seams toward the dark red fabric. *Place the Step 1 and Step 2 units in Bag 4.*

Make 24 of each.

Square in a Square Blocks

1. Using the Square in a Square method (page 43) and the Bag 3 pieces, make 17 bright blue/background Square in a Square blocks. These should measure 4½˝ × 4½˝. *Place in Bag 7.*

Make 17.

2. Make 6 dark red/background Square in a Square blocks using the Bag 3 pieces. *Place in Bag 4.*

Make 6.

Small Star Blocks

1. Use the small yellow squares, the dark red/yellow Flying Geese, and the dark red squares in Bag 4 to create 6 small star blocks. Lay out a template layer (page 22), making sure that each part is turned properly, and then stack the remaining parts on top.

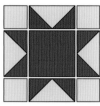

Small star assembly—make 6.

2. Assembly-line sew (page 23) the left vertical seams. Flip-flop press the seams (page 40) toward the dark red fabric.

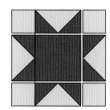

Sew the seams on the left side.

3. Assembly-line sew the right vertical seams. Press toward the dark red.

4. Sew the cross seams. Press. These 6 blocks should measure 8½˝ × 8½˝. *Place in Bag 5.*

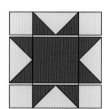

Sew the right-hand seams.

5. Repeat Steps 1–4 to make 6 blocks with the small orange squares, background/orange Flying Geese, and dark red Square in a Square blocks from Bag 4. Press toward the orange. *Place the 6 blocks in Bag 5.*

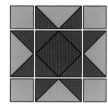

Make 6.

Big Star Blocks

Using the Bag 5 pieces and following the same steps as for the small star blocks (page 74), make 6 *each* of orange stars and yellow stars. These blocks should measure 16½˝ × 16½˝. Set them aside for now. You're nearly done!

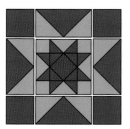 

Big star assembly—make 6 of each.

Connecting Corners

1. Take the 24 lemon yellow 2½˝ × 2½˝ squares and 12 of the background 6½˝ × 4½˝ rectangles from Bag 6. Align a lemon yellow square on a corner of the background rectangle so the drawn line cuts across the corner. Sew on the line. Trim away the excess corner fabric and press the seam toward the lemon yellow triangle. Repeat with the 11 remaining background rectangles.

Sew the corners, trim, and press.

2. Place a lemon yellow square on the corner next to the one you just sewed. Repeat Step 1, sewing on the line, trimming, and pressing. *Place in Bag 7.*

Add a second connecting corner. Make 12.

3. Repeat Steps 1 and 2 with the 24 dark yellow 2½˝ × 2½˝ squares and the remaining 12 background 6½˝ × 4½˝ rectangles. *Place the finished units in Bag 7.*

Make 12.

Sashing

You're coasting down to the big finish, but first it's time to put together the sashing strips using the pieces in Bag 7. You have three different color placements.

1. Join a dark yellow/background rectangle, a bright blue Square in a Square, and a plain background rectangle end to end, as shown. Make 5.

Sew together end to end. Make 5.

2. Repeat Step 1 with the lemon yellow/background rectangles. Make 5 of these.

Repeat with the lemon yellow pieced units. Make 5.

3. Repeat Step 1 once more with the lemon yellow/background rectangles, bright blue Square in a Square units, and dark yellow/background rectangles. Make 7.

Make 7.

4. Because the pieced sashing rectangles have so many different color placements, it's safest to lay out all the blocks and sashing rectangles to make sure everything is in the correct position. Sewing and pressing the blocks one at a time will eliminate confusion.

Lay out the blocks and sashing.

5. Referring to the instructions in Sashing As You Go (page 28), add the sashing and cornerstones from Bag 7 to the blocks.

6. Sew a 4½˝ × 36½˝ background fabric segment to a 4½˝ × 40½˝ background fabric segment. Press the seam. Make 2. These are the side borders.

7. Sew a 4½˝ × 24½˝ background fabric segment to a 4½˝ × 40½˝ background fabric segment. Press the seam. Make 2. These are the top and bottom borders.

8. Sew the side borders in place and press the seams toward the border. Then sew on the top and bottom borders.

Quilt assembly diagram

- -

Finishing the Quilt

Refer to The Big Finish (page 50) for guidelines on layering, quilting, blocking, and binding your quilt.

oopsie daisies

FINISHED SIZE: 66″ × 86½″

Designed, pieced, and quilted by Beth Ferrier

Don't you love it when a quilt makes you smile? This is such a happy design. Consider making all yellow flowers with brown centers for sunflowers, or use reds and oranges with black centers for poppies. The possibilities are endless!

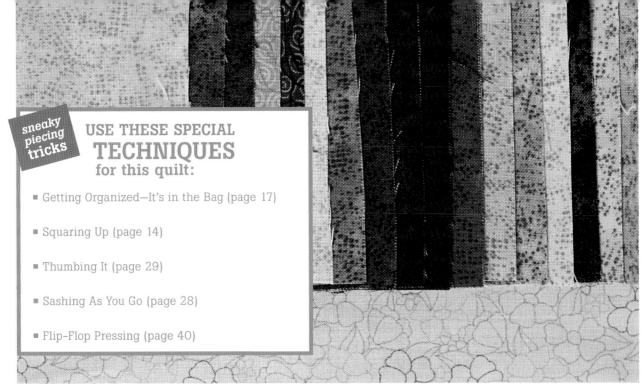

USE THESE SPECIAL
TECHNIQUES
for this quilt:

- Getting Organized—It's in the Bag (page 17)

- Squaring Up (page 14)

- Thumbing It (page 29)

- Sashing As You Go (page 28)

- Flip-Flop Pressing (page 40)

Fabrics used in this quilt

materials

Yardage is based on 40˝-wide fabric. Yardage amounts have been rounded up to include a little wiggle room.

2 coordinating fat eighths (about 9˝ × 20˝) in each of 6 different flower colors for a total of 12

6 fat quarters (about 18˝ × 20˝) in assorted greens for leaves

½ yard yellow fabric for flower centers

4⅝ yards background fabric

Backing fabric and batting sized for quilt

6 gallon-size zip-top plastic bags, labeled 1–6

Rotary cutter, mat, and ruler (6˝ or 6½˝ square is handy.)

14 yards medium rickrack trim in assorted greens

Quilter's ¼˝ tape (*Place in Bag 5.*)

Water-soluble gluestick

cutting

WOF = width of fabric

As you cut, you'll organize your cut pieces into bags as indicated.

fat-eighth flower fabrics

Cut 3 squares 6¼˝ × 6¼˝ from *each* of 12 fat eighths. Cut these on the diagonal *twice* (to make quarter-square triangles) and pin coordinating colors together. *Place in Bag 3.*

Cut 4 squares 2˝ × 2˝ from *each* fabric. *Place in Bag 4.*

fat-quarter leaf fabrics

Cut 2 strips 3˝ × about 20˝ from each of 6 fat quarters. Subcut:

 4 rectangles 3˝ × 4½˝ from each fabric.
 4 rectangles 3˝ × 2½˝ from each fabric. *Place all in Bag 1.*

Cut 2 strips 2¾˝ × about 20˝ from each of 6 fat quarters. Subcut:

 4 rectangles 2¾˝ × 5˝ from each fabric.
 4 squares 2¾˝ × 2¾˝ from each fabric. *Place all in Bag 2.*

flower center fabrics

Cut 2 strips 5½" × WOF. Subcut:

   12 squares 5½" × 5½". *Place in Bag 4.*

background fabric

Cut 4 strips 16½" × WOF. Subcut:

   31 rectangles 16½" × 5". *Place in Bag 6.*
   4 squares 4" × 4". *Place in Bag 5.*

Cut 2 strips 8" × WOF. Subcut:

   12 rectangles 8" × 4½". *Place in Bag 1.*
   8 squares 4" × 4". *Place in Bag 5.*

Cut 2 strips 6¼" × WOF. Subcut:

   12 squares 6¼" × 6¼". Cut these on
   the diagonal *twice* (to make quarter-
   square triangles). *Place in Bag 3.*

Cut 4 strips 4½" × WOF. Subcut:

   36 rectangles 4½" × 4". *Place in Bag 1.*
   4 squares 4" × 4". *Place in Bag 5.*

Cut 4 strips 4" × WOF. Subcut:

   32 squares 4" × 4". *Place in Bag 5.*
   Cut the remainder of the last strip
   to 3" × about 30". Subcut:
   12 rectangles 3" × 2½". *Place in Bag 1.*

Cut 1 strip 3" × WOF. Subcut:

   12 rectangles 3" × 2½". *Place in Bag 1.*

Cut 2 strips 2¾" × WOF. Subcut:

   24 squares 2¾" × 2¾". *Place in Bag 2.*

Cut 9 strips 2" × WOF for the
binding. *Place in Bag 6.*

rickrack

Cut 12 segments, each 7" long. *Place in Bag 1.*

Cut 12 segments, each 10" long. *Place in Bag 1.*

Cut 24 segments, each 5" long. *Place in Bag 2.*

Cut 12 segments, each 12" long. *Place in Bag 5.*

Instructions

*Unless otherwise noted, all seam allow-
ances are ¼", and pieces are sewn right sides
together. Seams are always pressed away
from the background (AFTB).*

Block Leaves

Use the pieces in Bag 1 to make mirror-
image block leaves.

1. Start with the right-side leaves. Sew
the 3" × 2½" leaf and background fabric
rectangles together along a 3" side. The
leaf fabric should be on the right. Catch a 7"
length of rickrack in the top of the seam at a
45° angle, as shown. Press the seam toward
the leaf fabric. Make 12.

Catch the rick-
rack in the seam.
Make 12.

2. Sew a 3" × 4½" leaf fabric rectangle to
the top edge of each Step 1 unit. These
blocks should measure 5½" × 4½". Roll up
the rickrack, and pin it to the block to make
the next few rounds of piecing easier.

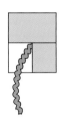

Sew a rectangle
to the top.

3. Sew a 4½" × 4" background fabric rectangle to the top and bottom of each block.
Press carefully. These should measure
4½" × 12½". *Place in Bag 5.*

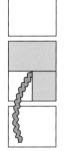

Add background
squares at both
ends.

4. Repeat Steps 1 and 2, but this time place the leaf fabric on the left, with a 10″ length of rickrack caught at the top of the seam. Press. Make 12.

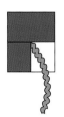

Reverse the fabric and trim direction. Make 12.

5. Sew a 4½″ × 4″ background fabric rectangle to the top and an 8″ × 4½″ background fabric rectangle to the bottom. Press. These should measure 4½″ × 16½″. *Place in Bag 5.*

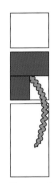

Sew rectangles to each end.

Cornerstone Leaves

These blocks are made just as before, except there are no rights and lefts to worry about! Using Bag 2, make 24. That's 4 more than you'll actually need, but it's nice to have a few extra to help distribute the different fabrics more evenly.

1. Sew together the 2¾″ × 2¾″ leaf and background fabric squares, catching a 5″ piece of rickrack at a 45° angle at the top of the seam. Press the seams AFTB. Make 24.

Join the squares, catching rickrack in the seam.

2. Sew one of the remaining leaf fabric 2¾″ × 5″ rectangles to the top edge (where the rickrack is caught) of each pieced rectangle. Press.

Add a rectangle to the top.

3. Using matching (or contrasting, if desired) thread, topstitch the rickrack in place. Feel free to curve it whatever way makes you happy. A little smear of glue on the wrong side of the rickrack will hold it in position while you are stitching. (But let the glue dry first, or it will gum up the sewing machine needle.) Trim the excess even with the edge of the block. *Place in Bag 6.*

Hourglass Blocks

Using the pieces in Bag 3, make simple Hourglass blocks. Fabric placement is critical, so work through the steps with a single color pair at a time.

1. Select 8 same flower-color triangles, 4 triangles of its coordinate color, and 4 triangles of the background fabric.

2. Arrange the triangles so that 2 flower-color triangles face each other. Add a background triangle and a coordinating flower triangle facing it. Use this template layer to stack the remaining triangles to create 4 Hourglass blocks.

Arrange the triangles.

3. Assembly-line sew (page 23) the triangles together and flip-flop press (page 40) the seams AFTB. Sew the cross seam and press. Make 4 square blocks, each 5½″ × 5½″.

4. Trim the blocks to 5½″ × 4″ by cutting away the side that's mostly the coordinate fabric. Sneaky, eh? Pin the 4 rectangles together and *place in Bag 5.*

Cut off one edge of the square.

5. Using the same flower and coordinate fabrics, but this time with their positions swapped, repeat Steps 1–4. This time the flower fabric will end up as the little triangle, and its coordinate fabric will be the petals.

6. Repeat Steps 1–5 for all 6 of the flower/coordinate fabric pairs. *Place all in Bag 5.*

Center Square Units

Use the pieces in Bag 4 to make this version of the traditional Snowball block. The Connecting Corners technique (page 27) makes short work of these. The corner fabric in each square matches up with one of the Hourglass units you've just made. As each square is finished, pin it to a corresponding stack of trimmed Hourglass units in Bag 5.

1. Start with 4 matching flower fabric 2″ × 2″ squares. On the wrong side of each, draw a diagonal line to divide each square in half.

2. Place each flower fabric square on a corner of a flower center 5½″ × 5½″ square, with the diagonal line cutting across the corner.

Place a square in each corner.

3. Sew on the lines and trim away the excess, leaving a ¼″ seam allowance. Press the seams away from the flower center.

Stitch across the corners and trim.

4. Repeat Steps 1–3 with each set of flower fabric squares. Hang onto these blocks for Assembling the Blocks.

- -

Assembling the Blocks

Gather the pieces from Bag 5 and the center square units to make the 12 flower heads. These are just uneven nine-patches—easy peasy.

1. Collect the parts for 1 flower: 4 trimmed Hourglass blocks, 1 coordinating center Snowball block, and 4 background fabric 4″ × 4″ squares. Pin a 12″ length of rickrack to the inside corner of a background square; it doesn't matter which one, as long as it's positioned so the rickrack tucks under the flower.

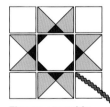

Flower assembly diagram

2. Sew the left vertical seam. Use Sneaky Trick: Thumbing It (page 29) to make sure the small triangles cross at the seamline. Flip-flop press the seams AFTB.

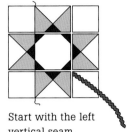

Start with the left vertical seam.

3. Sew the right vertical seam, aligning as in Step 2. Press AFTB.

4. Sew the cross seams. Press AFTB. The block should measure 12½″ × 12½″ at this point.

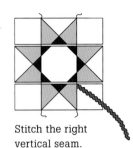

Stitch the right vertical seam.

5. Sew a right leaf rectangle to the same side of the flower block as the rickrack. Press the seams toward the leaf rectangle.

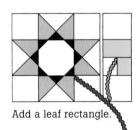

Add a leaf rectangle.

6. Sew a left leaf rectangle to the bottom of the block. Press the seam toward the leaf rectangle. The block should measure 16½″ × 16½″.

7. Repeat Steps 1–6 for the remaining 11 sets of flower parts.

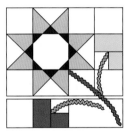

Attach a second leaf rectangle.

8. Position the rickrack stems as desired using the gluestick to hold them. Topstitch the stems in place.

Sashing

Play with the placement of all the beautiful flower blocks, twisting and turning them until they all look happy. Refer to Sneaky Trick: Sashing as You Go (page 28) and add the sashing strips and leaf block cornerstones from Bag 6.

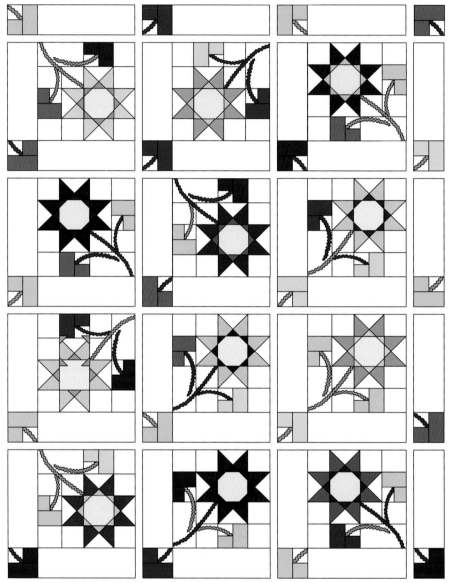

Arrange the flowers as you like and add the sashing.

Finishing the Quilt

Refer to The Big Finish (page 50) for guidelines on layering, quilting, blocking, and binding your quilt.

sur la table

FINISHED SIZE: 42″ × 42″

Designed, pieced, and quilted by Beth Ferrier

There are so many sneaky piecing tricks stuffed into this charming little quilt! Make just one of these, and you'll be an expert. Make four and you'll have a queen-sized quilt.

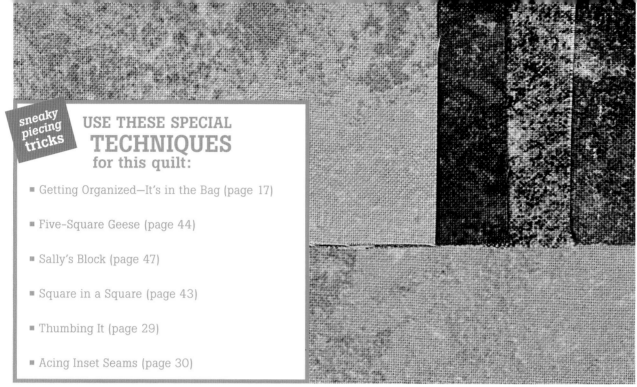

sneaky piecing tricks

USE THESE SPECIAL
TECHNIQUES
for this quilt:

- Getting Organized—It's in the Bag (page 17)

- Five-Square Geese (page 44)

- Sally's Block (page 47)

- Square in a Square (page 43)

- Thumbing It (page 29)

- Acing Inset Seams (page 30)

materials

Yardage is based on 40˝-wide fabric. Yardage amounts have been rounded up to include a little wiggle room.

1½ yards background fabric for blocks and binding

⅝ yard teal fabric for blocks

⅝ yard green fabric for blocks

⅝ yard purple fabric for blocks

¼ yard periwinkle fabric for blocks

Backing fabric and batting sized for quilt

6 gallon-size zip-top plastic bags, labeled 1–6

Rotary cutter, mat, and ruler (12½˝ square recommended)

Quilter's ¼˝ tape *(Place in Bag 5.)*

4¾˝ square of template plastic, optional *(Place in Bag 3.)*

Marking pencil

cutting

WOF = width of fabric

As you cut, you'll organize your cut pieces into bags as indicated.

background fabric

Cut 1 strip 11¼˝ × WOF. Subcut:

    1 square 11¼˝ × 11¼˝. Cut on the diagonal *twice* (to make quarter-square triangles). *Place in Bag 5.*

    Cut the remainder of the strip into 2 strips, 1 at 7½˝ × about 28˝ and 1 at 3½˝ × about 28˝. Subcut:

        3 squares 7½˝ × 7½˝. *Place in Bag 5.*

        1 segment 3½˝ × 24½˝. *Place in Bag 6.*

Cut 1 strip 7¼˝ × WOF. Subcut:

    2 squares 7¼˝ × 7¼˝. *Place in Bag 2.*

    Cut the remainder of the strip into 2 strips, 1 at 3⅞˝ × about 25˝ and 1 at 2˝ × about 25˝. Subcut:

        6 squares 3⅞˝ × 3⅞˝. *Place in Bag 3.*

        1 segment 2˝ × about 25˝ for the binding. *Place in Bag 6.*

Cut 1 strip 4½˝ × WOF. Subcut:

    1 segment 4½˝ × 14˝. *Place in Bag 4.*

    6 squares 3⅞˝ × 3⅞˝. *Place in Bag 3.*

Cut 2 strips 3⅞″ × WOF. Subcut:

12 squares 3⅞″ × 3⅞″. *Place 4 in Bag 3.* Mark the remaining 8 squares in half diagonally on the wrong side. *Place in Bag 2.*

1 segment 3½″ × 24½″. *Place in Bag 6.*

Cut 3 strips 3½″ × WOF. Subcut:

1 segment 3½″ × 24½″. *Place in Bag 6.*

2 segments 3½″ × 30½″. *Place in Bag 6.*

4 squares 2½″ × 2½″. *Place in Bag 1.*

Cut 1 strip 10″ × WOF. Subcut:

1 square 7½″ × 7½″. *Place in Bag 5.*

Cut the remainder of the strip into 5 strips, each 2″ × about 32″ for the binding. *Place in Bag 6.*

teal fabric

Cut 2 strips 3″ × WOF. *Place in Bag 5.*

Cut 1 strip 3½″ × WOF. Subcut:

1 segment 3½″ × 14″. *Place in Bag 4.*

4 rectangles 2½″ × 4½″. *Place in Bag 1.*

green fabric

Cut 1 strip 3″ × WOF. *Place in Bag 5.*

Cut 1 strip 7¼″ × WOF. Subcut:

2 squares 7¼″ × 7¼″. *Place in Bag 2.*

4 rectangles 4½″ × 2½″. *Place in Bag 1.*

Cut 1 strip 3⅞″ × WOF. Subcut:

8 squares 3⅞″ × 3⅞″. Mark the diagonal on the wrong side. *Place in Bag 2.*

purple fabric

Cut 1 strip 3″ × WOF. *Place in Bag 5.*

Cut 1 strip 6½″ × WOF. Subcut:

2 rectangles 6½″ × 7½″. *Place in Bag 4.*

4 rectangles 4½″ × 2½″. *Place in Bag 1.*

Cut 1 strip 4¾″ × WOF. Subcut:

8 squares 4¾″ × 4¾″. *Place in Bag 3.*

periwinkle fabric

Cut 1 strip 3″ × WOF. *Place in Bag 5.*

Cut 1 strip 2½″ × WOF. Subcut:

4 rectangles 2½″ × 4½″. *Place in Bag 1.*

Instructions

Unless otherwise noted, all seam allowances are ¼″, and pieces are sewn right sides together. Seams are always pressed away from the background (AFTB).

Partial-Seam Blocks

Make 4 blocks as illustrated, using the pieces in Bag 1 and following the instructions for Sewing Partial Seams (page 30). Position the fabrics around the center square however you like. The blocks should measure 6½″ × 6½″. *Place in Bag 2.*

Make 4 blocks.

Flying Geese

Use Sneaky Trick: Five-Square Geese (page 44) to make these blocks with the pieces in Bag 2.

1. Make 8 units using the small background fabric squares and the large green squares.

2. Make 8 more units the same way, using the small green squares and the large background squares.

Flying Geese—
Make 8 of each.

3. Sew a goose from Step 1 to a goose from Step 2, with the large green triangle touching the small green triangles to form a chevron shape. Press the seams toward the large green triangles. These units should measure 6½″ × 6½″. Make 8.

Connect Flying Geese to form a chevron shape. Make 8.

4. Sew the large background-triangle side of these units to opposite sides of the partial seam units finished earlier, as shown. Press the seams toward the partial seam unit. *Place in Bag 3.*

Sew 2 squares to a partial-seam unit. Make 4.

Square in a Square

Make 8 blocks using the pieces in Bag 3. Refer to Sneaky Trick: Square in a Square (page 43) for the trimming and sewing sequence and for instructions on making an optional trim template.

Square in a square

1. Arrange the background fabric squares into stacks of 8. Cut in half on the diagonal. Use the folding and chopping technique or the optional plastic template to make quick work of trimming all the triangles you need for the blocks.

Trim the triangles for the blocks.

2. Using the trimmed triangles and the purple squares, make 8 Square in a Square blocks that measure 6½″ × 6½″.

3. Sew a block to each end of the 8 Flying Geese blocks. Press the seams whichever direction looks better. *Place in Bag 4.*

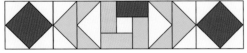

Attach the square in a square units.

Sally's Block

Make 4 blocks using the pieces in Bag 4. Refer to Sneaky Trick: Sally's Block (page 47). The blocks should measure 6½″ × 6½″. Sew a block to each end of 2 of the border strips in the bag. Make sure the block is oriented properly. *Place in Bag 6.*

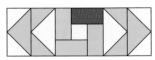

Sally's block

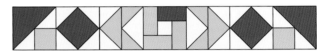

Add blocks to the ends of 2 border strips.

Lone Star Block

Use the pieces from Bag 5 to make the strip sets for the Lone Star blocks in this quilt. To have the fabrics show up where you want in the star, pay careful attention to how the strips are sewn together. Offsetting the beginning of the strip set lets you cut more efficiently.

1. Sew purple and teal strips together for Strip Set 1 so that the purple is on top, extending about 3″ to the left of the teal. Press the seams toward the purple.

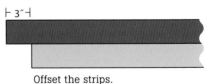

Offset the strips.

2. Establish a 45° angle and make the first cut. Keeping your ruler at that angle, measure 3″ from the bias edge and cut 8 segments.

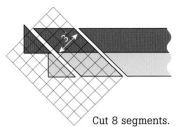

Cut 8 segments.

3. Use teal and periwinkle strips to make Strip Set 2. First, cut the strips in half crosswise to a length of about 20″, then proceed as in Steps 1 and 2 with half-length strips. Place the teal on top, extending out about 3″. Press the seams toward the periwinkle. Cut 4 segments.

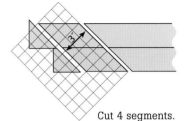

Cut 4 segments.

4. Use the remaining half strip of teal with half the green strip for Strip Set 3. The teal should be on top again, extending to the left. Press the seams toward the green. Cut 4 segments.

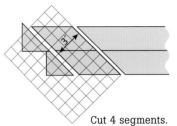

Cut 4 segments.

5. To make Pieced Diamond 1, take a segment each from Strip Sets 1 and 2. Layer the segments, right sides together, with Strip Set 2 on top. Use Sneaky Trick: Thumbing It (page 29) to position the seams for a perfect intersection. Repeat and assembly-line sew (page 23) to make 4 diamonds. Press carefully to avoid distorting the shapes.

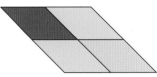

Pieced Diamond 1—
make 4.

6. To make Pieced Diamond 2, repeat Step 5 with the remaining Strip Set 1 segments and the Strip Set 3 segments. Make 4.

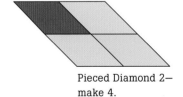

Pieced Diamond 2—
make 4.

7. Following the directions for Acing Inset Seams (page 30), complete the Lone Star block using the 8 pieced diamonds, 4 background squares, and 4 triangles from Bag 5. The finished block should measure 24½″ × 24½″. Trim to size if necessary, being careful to leave a ¼″ seam allowance outside each diamond point.

Lone Star block

Borders and Binding

1. Using the pieces in Bag 6, sew the shorter (3½˝ × 24½˝) background strips to opposite sides of the Lone Star block. Press.

2. Sew the longer (3½˝ × 30½˝) background strips to the remaining sides of the block. Press.

3. Sew the shorter pieced border strips to the sides with the shoter background strips. Press the seams toward the pieced border.

Attach the shorter border strips first.

4. Sew the longer pieced border strips to the remaining edges of the quilt top. Press the seams toward the pieced border.

Quilt top assembly diagram

Finishing the Quilt

Refer to The Big Finish (page 50) for guidelines on layering, quilting, blocking, and binding your quilt.

mardi gras

FINISHED SIZE: 19½″ × 58½″

Pull out all the stops! This project is designed to showcase our mad piecing skills. Set diagonally—on point— the pieced setting triangles can be used with any block that finishes at 12″ × 12″. Hang this quilt as a banner, or display it as a table runner.

Designed, pieced, and quilted by Beth Ferrier

Fabrics used in this quilt

materials

*Yardage is based on 40″-wide fabric.
Yardage amounts have been rounded
up to include a little wiggle room.*

⅞ yard background fabric
for pieced blocks

½ yard red fabric for pieced
blocks and binding

1 fat quarter (about 18″ × 20″)
orange fabric for pieced blocks

1 fat quarter (about 18″ × 20″)
green fabric for pieced blocks

½ yard bright blue fabric
for pieced blocks

Backing fabric and batting sized for quilt

6 gallon-size zip-top bags, labeled 1–6

Rotary cutter, mat, and ruler (12½″
square would be handy.)

Quilter's ¼″ tape (*Place in Bag 4.*)

8 squares water-soluble paper,
about 2″ × 2″ (*Place in Bag 1.*)

Marking pencil

cutting

WOF = width of fabric

*As you cut, you'll organize your cut
pieces into bags as indicated.*

background fabric

Cut 2 strips 11″ × WOF.

From the first strip, subcut:

3 squares 11″ × 11″. Cut in half *twice*
on the diagonal. *Place in Bag 4.*

4 squares 2⅞″ × 2⅞″. Cut in half
diagonally. *Place in Bag 3.*

From the second strip, subcut:

1 square 11″ × 11″. Cut in half *twice*
on the diagonal. *Place in Bag 4.*

From the remainder, subcut:

1 strip 5⅜″ × about 29″.

1 strip 2⅞″ × about 29″.

From the 5⅜″ strip, subcut:

8 rectangles 5⅜″ × 2⅝″. *Place in Bag 1.*

2 squares 3½″ × 3½″. *Place in Bag 5.*

From the 2⅞″ strip, subcut:

8 squares 2⅞″ × 2⅞″. Cut in half on the diagonal. *Place in Bag 2.*

Cut 1 strip 4¼″ × WOF. Subcut:

4 squares 4¼″ × 4¼″. Cut in half on the diagonal. *Place in Bag 5.*

6 squares 3½″ × 3½″. *Place in Bag 5.*

red fabric

Cut 2 strips 2″ × WOF. Fold in half, wrong sides together. Using the diamond template (page 94), cut into 16 diamonds—8 and 8 reversed. *Place in Bag 2.*

Cut 5 strips 2″ × WOF for the binding. *Place in Bag 6.*

Cut 2 squares 5¼″ × 5¼″. *Place in Bag 5.*

orange fabric

Cut 2 strips 2⅞″ × about 20″. Subcut:

8 squares 2⅞″ × 2⅞″. Cut in half on the diagonal. *Place in Bag 2.*

Cut 2 strips 3⅞″ × about 20″. Subcut:

8 squares 3⅞″ × 3⅞″. Mark in half on the diagonal on the wrong side. *Place in Bag 5.*

green fabric

Cut 1 strip 2⅞″ × about 20″. Subcut:

4 squares 2⅞″ × 2⅞″. Cut in half on the diagonal. *Place in Bag 3.*

Cut 1 strip 3⅞″ × about 20″. Subcut:

4 squares 3⅞″ × 3⅞″. Cut in half on the diagonal. *Place in Bag 5.*

bright blue fabric

Cut 1 strip 4⅞″ × WOF. Using the kite template (page 94), cut the strip into 8 kite shapes. *Place in Bag 1.*

Cut 2 squares 4¾″ × 4¾″. *Place in Bag 5.*

Instructions

Unless otherwise noted, all seam allowances are ¼″, and pieces are sewn right sides together. Seams are always pressed away from the background fabric (AFTB).

Spiky Points

Make 8 units, using the pieces in Bag 1.

1. Neatly stack the background fabric rectangles, 2 right side up and 2 wrong side up. Cut the stack in half diagonally. Use the skinny background triangle trim template (page 94) to cut away the points. Repeat to cut the remaining 4 rectangles.

2. Lay out a template layer (page 22) of a kite shape, a right background triangle, and a left background triangle. All the skinny points should meet in a corner. Stack the remaining pieces on top.

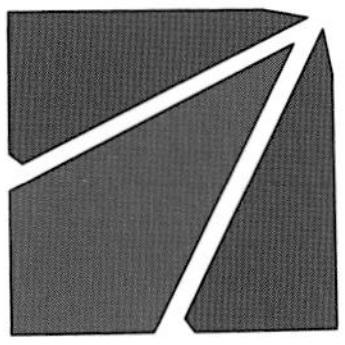

Make a template layer.

3. Complete a kite block following Steps 4 and 5 (below) to make sure it ends up 4½″ × 4½″. Adjust your seam allowance as needed. Then assembly-line sew the remaining kites. Press the seams away from the background fabric. Leave on the paper for now. Make 8.

4. Align a right triangle with a kite shape, right sides together. (See how your nipped-off points make it easy to position the background triangle?) Sewing onto a piece of water-soluble paper (page 26) for a few stitches, tip the skinny points under the presser foot and stitch.

Stitch together, supporting the points with water-soluble paper.

5. Using the notched corner opposite the skinny point, align the remaining background triangles with the other side of the kites. Assembly-line sew (page 23) them. Press the seams away from the background. These little gems have super-stretchy biases; take extra care with pressing. It will be lovely if they measure 4½″ × 4½″. *Place in Bag 4.*

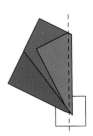

Attach the second triangle.

Diamonds

Using the pieces in Bag 2, make 8 right-leaning and 8 left-leaning diamond units.

Right and left diamonds

1. Start with the right-leaning diamonds. Place an orange triangle along a long side of a diamond, right sides together, so that the top points match and a dog ear hangs off the bottom. Stitch. Press the seam toward the diamond.

Sew a triangle onto a diamond.

2. Sew a background triangle to the opposite side of the diamond. This time, align the points at the bottom, with the dog-ear going off the top. Press the seams AFTB. Make 8.

Add a background triangle on the other side.

3. Repeat Steps 1 and 2 with the left-leaning diamonds, first sewing on a background fabric triangle, then an orange triangle, and making 8. The units should measure 2½″ × 4½″. *Place in Bag 4.*

- -

Half-Square Triangles

Easy-peasy, lemon-squeezy! Sew together the triangles in Bag 3 to make 8 half-square triangle blocks, each 2½″ square. Press the seams AFTB. *Place in Bag 4.*

Setting Triangles

The corner block is just an uneven four-patch. But for really pretty intersections, check out Sneaky Trick: Thumbing It (page 29) to get the seams just right. Make 8 units from the Bag 4 pieces.

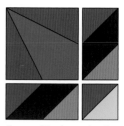

Corner block—make 8.

1. Lay out the template layer and stack the remaining pieces on top. Assembly-line sew the vertical seams, carefully aligning the kites and diamonds. Press the seams toward the kite fabric and toward the half-square triangle unit.

2. Repeat Step 1 with the cross seam. Once again, press toward the kite. These units should measure 6½″ square.

3. To show off your sharp points, the background setting triangles are oversized. The extra-large dog-ears let the piecing "float" on the background fabric. Align the right angle of a triangle with a corner of the pieced

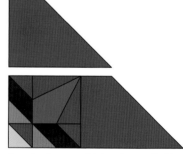

Sew background triangles on both sides of each pieced square. Make 8.

block; stitch. Press the seams toward the pieced block and trim away the dog ear. Repeat with another background triangle on the other side. Make 8. *Place in Bag 6.*

Tulip Geese

1. Sew Square in a Square blocks (page 43), using the Bag 5 pieces. Begin with the bright blue squares and the green triangles. Press the seams toward the bright blue square. The blocks should measure 6½″ × 6½″. Make 2. Set them aside for now.

2. Repeat Step 1, using the red squares and the background fabric triangles, to make 2 more blocks. These blocks should measure 7¼″ × 7¼″.

3. Use the 8 orange squares from Bag 5, the 2 background/red Square in a Square units from Step 2, and the Five-Square Geese technique (page 44) to create 8 Tulip Geese blocks. Press the seams toward the orange fabric. The geese should measure 3½″ × 6½″.

4. Use the 3½″ × 3½″ background fabric squares from Bag 5, the Tulip Geese, and the blue/green Square in a Square units from Step 1 to complete the center blocks. *Place in Bag 6.*

Square in a Square—make 2 of each.

Sew the Tulip Geese units. Make 8.

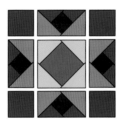

Center block assembly

Assembling the Quilt

Isn't it amazing what a little quarter-turn will do? Sew your blocks from Bag 6 together as always, except this time the seams will land on the diagonal. Give the piece a good pressing. Trim the edge, if necessary.

Quilt top assembly diagram

Finishing the Quilt
Refer to The Big Finish (page 50) for guidelines on layering, quilting, blocking, and binding your quilt.

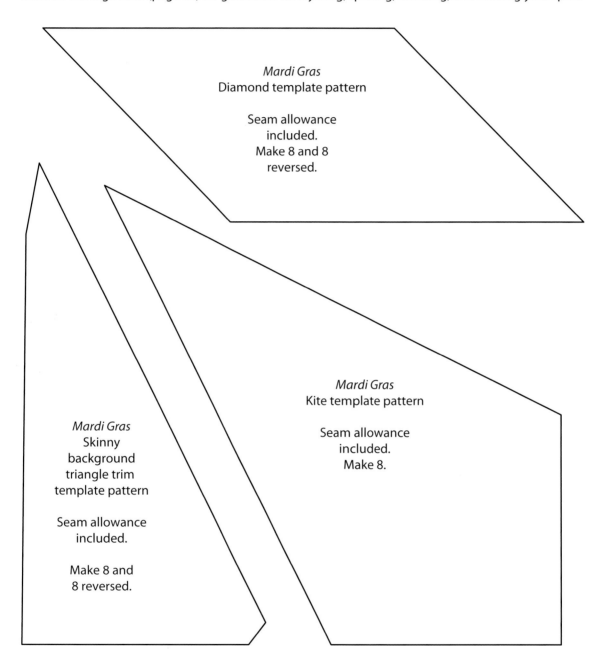

Mardi Gras
Diamond template pattern

Seam allowance
included.
Make 8 and 8
reversed.

Mardi Gras
Kite template pattern

Seam allowance
included.
Make 8.

Mardi Gras
Skinny
background
triangle trim
template pattern

Seam allowance
included.

Make 8 and
8 reversed.

resources

FABRICS

Northcott Fabrics
Essentials, Stonehenge,
and designs by Mark Lipinski
www.northcott.net

P&B Textiles
Designs by Beth Ferrier
www.pbtex.com

Red Rooster Fabrics
Tokyo
www.redroosterfabrics.com

Previous books and products by author:

about the author

Beth Ferrier's grandmother taught her to embroider when Beth was just four, setting her on a lifelong path of needlework. From then on, Beth's hands were always busy—knitting, sewing, weaving, making garments, first for her baby dolls and then for herself. She can't remember a time when fiber hasn't been a central part of her life.

She describes her style as "rebellious traditional." A quilter since 1975, she is forever in search of easy and simply elegant solutions to quilting challenges. Everything she designs is geared toward teaching skill-expanding tips and techniques.

Beth lives in Saginaw, Michigan, with her husband, Kent, in a farmhouse built before 1860. They have four grown sons, two daughters-in-law, and two grandchildren. You've seen her on *Simply Quilts*, *Kaye's Quilting Friends*, and *The Quilt Show* with Ricky Tims and Alex Anderson. She's written several books, most *recently More! Hand Appliqué by Machine* from C&T Publishing. Visit her website at www.applewoodfarmquilts.com.

Great Titles and Products

from C&T PUBLISHING

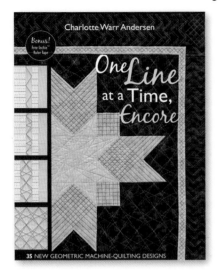

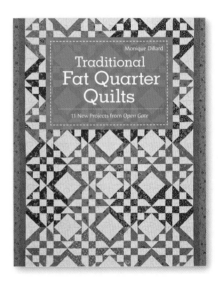

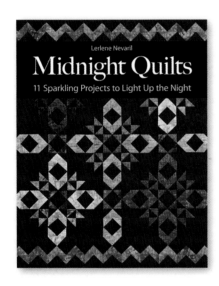

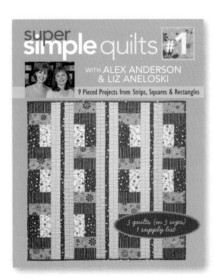

Available at your local retailer or **www.ctpub.com** *or* **800-284-1114**

For a list of other fine books from C&T Publishing, visit our website to view our catalog online.

C&T PUBLISHING, INC.

P.O. Box 1456
Lafayette, CA 94549
800-284-1114

Email: ctinfo@ctpub.com
Website: www.ctpub.com

C&T Publishing's professional photography services are now available to the public. Visit us at www.ctmediaservices.com.

Tips and Techniques can be found at www.ctpub.com > Consumer Resources > Quiltmaking Basics: Tips & Techniques for Quiltmaking & More

For quilting supplies:

COTTON PATCH

1025 Brown Ave.
Lafayette, CA 94549
Store: 925-284-1177
Mail order: 925-283-7883

Email: CottonPa@aol.com
Website: www.quiltusa.com

Note: Fabrics used in the quilts shown may not be currently available, as fabric manufacturers keep most fabrics in print for only a short time.